Contents

Preface

This book's Introduction begins by singling out some distinctive features of Martin Heidegger's account of truth, not only for the sake of a contrast with other philosophers, but also because he has said something that we need to hear, we who live in the twenty-first century and who read and think in English. The historical profiling of a philosopher is certainly valuable, but it is always more urgent to inquire what his work might mean to us in our own time.

After that first orientation, the Introduction will pinpoint one principal source for our study, one text (admittedly it exists in several versions) that will be submitted to a close reading in the body of this book. For I find that Heidegger's intricate compositions all need more individual attention than they have usually been given.

Then the introduction to Part I will outline what movements of thought there are in this text of Heidegger's, what course of questioning and answering it pursues. The reader who follows the "pathway of thinking" in the body of this book will discover there many distinctive facets of truth. The text we are studying exists in both an earlier and a later version, and that is why this book is divided into Part I and Part II.

The quotations from Heidegger will be drawn, wherever possible, from published English translations that the reader will find cited in the endnotes. But Part I will be devoted to early work on truth from 1930 that has only recently been published in German. I have translated this material and included the key passages in my text, together with an account of the movements of thought and the sources on which Heidegger drew. I hope that, by printing the quotations in boldface and indented, the text will encourage the reader to pause over them. Heidegger also offered two different lecture courses on Plato in the early 1930s that dealt centrally with truth; they are both available in English translation, but, to make sure that we not confuse them, I refer to them, not by title, but by the *date*, in boldface.

Acknowledgments

I am happy to acknowledge with gratitude the work of the late Walter Biemel, who did so much to pass along to later generations the substance of Heidegger's studies on truth. And I must acknowledge the generous teaching of his own contemporaries in phenomenology, Hans-Georg Gadamer and Paul Ricoeur, two outstanding philosophers in the generation after Heidegger. I want to express my gratitude to Friedrich-Wilhelm von Herrmann of Freiburg, whose writings and correspondence have helped direct my studies. Many members of the Heidegger Circle of North America have enlivened the current reception of his work, and given me all sorts of stimulation – I must particularly thank Babette Babich, Richard Capobianco, Richard Polt, and the indefatigable Thomas Sheehan, with whom I have often disagreed but who forced me, with cordiality, to look at the texts and the "things themselves" again and again. Closer to home, in the Toronto area, my wife Linda and I have enjoyed years of friendship and Heidegger discussion with Art Davis and Laurell Ritchie, Nelson Roland and Judith Levasseur, Bill Stratton and Suzanne Keppler. More recently, I have to thank Dieter Misgeld and Trevor Norris.

The philosophy editor at the University of Toronto Press, Len Husband, received several drafts of this book over a period of years and secured several appraisals that have proved very helpful to me. I am grateful for his patience and support. And it was Len who proposed the format of setting off the translated quotations in bold type, which I am sure readers will appreciate.

Key to References

Italics are used for German-language abbreviations.

EHP	*Elucidations of Hölderlin's Poetry*
GA 1–102	Heidegger's Collected Edition, *Gesamtausgabe*, vols. 1–102
(1930)	"On the Essence of Truth," December 1930 address in Freiburg, *GA* 80.1
Sec. I(a), Sec. I(b), etc.	Sections marked in the text of the (1930) Freiburg address
***WW* 1.1., etc.**	"On the Essence of Truth" (1943 and 1949), Chapter 1, first paragraph, etc.
SZ	*Being and Time*
SU, 3, etc.	"The Self-Assertion of the German University," third paragraph, etc.
PLT	Heidegger, *Poetry, Language, Thought*, ed. A. Hofstadter
31–32	Heidegger, *The Essence of Truth: On Plato's Parable of the Cave and the Theaetetus* (lectures, 1931–32)
33–34	Heidegger, *On the Essence of Truth* (lectures, 1933–34)
PLW	Heidegger, *Plato's Doctrine of Truth*
Contributions	*GA* 65 *Beiträge zur Philosophie*
WM	*What Is Metaphysics?*
Part I, Units 1–11	Chapters of this book, Part I
Part II, Units 1–13	Chapters of this book, Part II

HEIDEGGER ON TRUTH

Its Essence and Its Fate

Introduction

1. Truth, Untruth, and Heidegger

Inspired and guided by the phenomenological movement, Martin Heidegger approached the topic of truth as an element in our experience. He certainly recognized that our discourse was capable of being true or false, and that particular statements occurring in discourse could be true or false – and whenever he treats the topic of truth he is at pains to analyse and explain such instances. He shares that interest with many philosophers outside the phenomenological movement. But in addition, whenever he treats this topic he also points to a further dimension in which truth is found, and the present study will be concerned mainly with how he accomplishes that. In his phenomenology, we see that truth is the *medium* in which all human experience occurs. It shows itself in many other forms of language and speech beyond the statement, such as poetry; it is the crucial condition for perception, that is, for our encounter with things in the world; human conduct and human interactions are marked by truth or falsity, and so is our insertion in society and history.

The *medium* for experience – think of the analogy that Plato offered in the *Republic* 508: as light permits objects to be visible and the eye to see, so truth permits genuine beings to be intelligible and our *nous* to understand. Our study will show, in Part I, Unit 2, and Part II, Unit 2, how Heidegger recast the theory of knowledge that he had inherited from his teachers to move the topic of truth into the centre of things.

We shall focus on the work that Heidegger undertook in 1930 and later in a number of addresses and essays that had the title "On the Essence of Truth," *Vom Wesen der Wahrheit.* The addresses, offered on several occasions in 1930, have only just now been published,[1] and we shall offer an overview of them in Section (2) below, and then study them in Part I of this book. Heidegger himself published the final version in the form of an essay in German in 1949,[2] and an English translation of this version by John Sallis appeared in 1977 and again in 1998.[3] The essay will be our focus in Part II.

We may make an approach to the topic of truth by bringing forward three points about truth for which Heidegger is well known, all prominent themes in the addresses and essay. First, there is his preoccupation with what he sees as the usual concept of truth in philosophy, what the English-speaking world calls the "correspondence theory of truth." In this view, it is a statement (or proposition or sentence) that is declared to be true or false and that depends on whether it stands in *accord* with the subject matter it purports to address. In many different texts, including all our focus texts, Heidegger seeks to unravel what such according or corresponding could consist in; he also pays special attention to what makes accordance possible. We shall be following his manoeuvres with this "usual concept," but the upshot of the study is that it does not come close to exhausting the phenomenon of truth. Heidegger opens his discussion by confronting an antagonist (anti-philosophy) who says we cannot ask about the general nature of truth, because it is only *this* belief or *that* experience that can be true – always only this or that. We shall follow how he responds.

In the second place, an important testimony on truth, for Heidegger, is found among the very earliest Greek thinkers. The Greek word that we usually translate as "truth" is *alētheia*, and Heidegger accepts as the literal meaning of this word: "unconcealedness." The early Greek thinkers were astonished at the beings that came forward, displaying themselves in the open, and what became unconcealed there they called *physis*. For Heidegger, this is not merely an antiquarian point: though our experience is different from theirs, unconcealedness remains the essence of truth – and this point is expressed very eloquently in the essay we shall be studying. Certainly, this raises the question how the "usual concept" of truth, that is, correspondence of a statement and a thing, fits within this historic, ancient essence, and this is the key question we put to Heidegger through all the sections of this book. Another essay of Heidegger's, "The Origin of the Work of Art" (*UKW*, 1936),[4] gives a very impressive demonstration of the character of truth as unconcealedness. It makes the case that the work of art has truth in it, and this is marked by two features:

(a) In the work of art, truth *happens, geschieht*: it is an *event*, not a static correlation of the work to some subject external to it, like the resemblance of a portrait to the original. The work of art lets reality or being emerge in its unconcealedness.

> **There is here an occurring, a happening of truth at work ... So the nature of art would be this: the truth of beings setting itself to work.** (*PLT*, p. 36)

(b) The event of unconcealing has an inner, necessary connection to concealment. That implies that truth has an inner and necessary connection to untruth.

This essay was the harbinger of many studies Heidegger made of art and poetry later in the 1930s, 1940s, and 1950s, which were influential in encouraging currents of hermeneutical philosophy and poetics in all European countries after the Second World War.

In the third place is the negative aspect we just referred to in passing in point (b): the exploration of truth is only complete when we follow up the supplement, that *untruth* belongs to the essence of truth. In our focus essay, "On the Essence of Truth," this appears in two forms: first of all concealment (the privation of *alētheia*), and then the peculiarly human form of untruth: erring. We shall be seeing that it is the role of essence, *das Wesen*, in this analysis that brings these negative phenomena to the fore, and this is never more sharply displayed than in the present essay. And since truth is an element in all human experience, we shall be seeing that untruth, too, in all its forms, belongs essentially to our experience.

Even that brief summary is enough to allow us to point to two areas in which Heidegger's thought can help us today. First of all, we are inclined in daily life to confine the phenomenon of truth too narrowly. The public in modern times tends to believe that many occasions of speech are not subject to a rule or norm of truth at all. When we are joking, or "telling tales out of school," we don't expect to have to defend our utterances: the norm of truth is felt to be a *restriction* on our freedom of utterance that applies only in certain situations. This common feeling reflects the deeper commitment of our society to freedom of speech, but this principle is commonly understood in our society to be a freedom of self-expression. Free self-expression cannot be constrained by truth. We commonly believe in people's right to assert themselves, to raise their profile, to advance their interests, and, today, to seek publicity with a website. Where does truth fit in with all this? This question gains in urgency when we review the record of the social media, where not only individuals, but also groups and causes, sometimes anonymous or pseudonymous, disseminate messages to the world, and make war with rivals, free of any form of control or supervision. The system is saturated either with "fake news" or with repeated allegations of "fake news." It seems that in our times truth has become an issue of political debate in a completely new way: not only in determining what is true, but also in doubting whether politics and journalism can even be governed by it. Some people now say that the postmodern age is the "post-truth age."

We do not look to a philosopher to provide remedies for social problems, only to offer thoughts and words with which to comprehend them. And in this case, we can learn from Heidegger that truth is not a norm that operates only on certain occasions. Truth is pervasive in human experience, and Heidegger's description of experience recognizes how all of it is shaped by the phenomenon of truth. Centrally, this will include as well the pervasive phenomenon of untruth. The key contribution of Heidegger will be to show that truth does not stand over against freedom as some sort of restrictive norm, but is entirely fused with freedom and made possible by it. Where Heidegger differs from the common opinion I sketched above is that he does not treat our utterances as our self-expression, so he does not speak of a freedom of self-expression. Instead of that, he understands our freedom and our speech as our opening upon the world, endowed with the possibility of disclosing being, and there he locates the phenomenon of truth.

In the Conclusion of this book, I hope to show that treating the human being as *Da-sein* circumvents the idea that our speaking is self-expression.

What I shall stress in the second place is that Heidegger has sought to free the phenomenon of truth from restrictions that it suffered at the hands of previous philosophers. Usually, they located this topic within the theory of knowledge – in practice, the theory of science. This philosophy would treat scientific reasoning with the apparatus of modern logic, so that truth as well was expounded in logical terms. There were debates about what constituted truth, but it was generally conceded that a singular statement *p* was, in each case, the truth-bearer, the proper subject of "true" or "false."

Heidegger, however, shows that truth is pervasive within human experience. Yes, it applies to statements, but also to perception, conduct, and every phenomenon of our existence. By overcoming in this way the restrictiveness of the logical-analytical account of truth, Heidegger prepares us to reconsider the status of "sciences" as over against other research-and-education initiatives of the academy. The logical restriction of truth certainly had the effect of separating the "sciences" (now called STEM) from the humanistic disciplines of the university. Positivists and empiricists often tried to apply their concept of truth to those disciplines, but without success, leading to the dismal conclusion that truth is never found in such disciplines.

Throughout his work, Heidegger returns again and again to analysis of the sciences and other academic disciplines, where his principal guide is the phenomenon of truth. We shall be quoting from time to time his early work on science, still neo-Kantian in spirit, and then looking in more detail at the treatments he gives to *all* the academic disciplines, scientific and otherwise, in the 1920s and later, studies in a phenomenological spirit that expressed his work on truth and the essence of truth. Indeed, all of this work came to a kind of climax in the early 1930s, when he sought to give practical expression to his views on the academic disciplines by undertaking university reform during his period as Rector of the University of Freiburg, 1933–34. His thoughts on the university also sprang from his earlier work on knowledge and truth. But history brought him into a conjuncture with German politics in 1933–34 that was calamitous for him and for which he was utterly unprepared. Trying to master the forces that were driving the university, he was led into a political adventure with the National Socialists that, for many commentators, has come to define his historic role. I do not at all avoid the question of Heidegger's politics in this book, but I see it as an intermission in his life, preceded and followed by concentrated philosophical work. His political connections arose out of his efforts to reform the university in accord with his understanding of knowledge and truth. Then, grasping to some degree where he had gone astray, and sensing how some elements of his early philosophy of truth had led him there, he undertook after 1934 to correct his own course. Those corrections appear most clearly in the 1949 published version of his essay "On the Essence of Truth." The entanglement of academic disciplines and politics is treated below in the Intermission after Part I.

Both Parts I and II of this book should be of help to students working on the early texts on truth, on the 1949 essay, on Heidegger's Plato lectures of the 1930s, on "The Origin of the Work of Art," and on his *Contributions to Philosophy.* Beyond that, I hope that all readers will find that the topic of truth in Heidegger leads quite naturally into the other main themes of his thinking, and that these themes take on a particular clarity and coherence when they are approached from the angle of the essence of truth. Part I, Unit 7, treats the character of human existence; our status as *Da-sein* is treated in Part I, Unit 7, and Part II, Unit 6; the entire theme of being comes to the fore in Part I, Unit 6, and Part II, Units 4, 5 and 6.

2. Heidegger's Texts on Truth

Heidegger's best-known work, the 1927 book *Being and Time* (*SZ*),[5] focuses on the ontological constitution of ourselves, human beings, as *Existenz.* In *SZ,* truth is intimately linked to existence. Section 44 shows how our statements accomplish truth through our uncovering, *Entdecken,* of things in the environment; then 44(b) traces several further strata of truth within our existence: our perception and conduct are likewise engaged in uncovering the things in our environment; these things that are uncovered are showing themselves thereby in their truth; our existence reveals to us the character of our own being; all of these disclosures are made possible by the disclosure of the world, the primordial truth. Here we refer the reader to other treatments of *SZ*, my earlier article,[6] and Dahlstrom's major book,[7] which shows that since the phenomenon of truth is not confined to statements, philosophy should never have domesticated it within a logical or linguistic frame, what he has appropriately called the "logical prejudice." The present study of the essence of truth is focused rather on the work from 1930 and 1949 but will frequently refer back to *SZ* to explicate the connections and differences.

Later, I shall quote from the lecture course of 1925–26 at the University of Marburg, *Logic: The Question of Truth.*[8] Looking further back among the lectures in Marburg, we find the course from 1924–25, now published as *Plato's Sophist*,[9] which offers a very full and very early account of several Greek texts on truth, and which I treated in a separate publication.[10] Shortly after the publication of *SZ*, there were a number of other lecture courses that dealt with aspects of the question of truth, and we shall be considering them as our study proceeds. But one group of texts by title and content needs to stand at the centre of our attention, texts called "On the Essence of Truth" *(WW)*.

There were four occasions in 1930 on which Heidegger delivered oral addresses under this title: in Karlsruhe (14 July), Bremen (8 October), Marburg (5 December), and Freiburg (11 December).[11] Many years then elapsed between the original conception of the work and its first publication (1943 – an edition that appeared in an earlier English translation in 1949[12]) and its second publication (1949). Now separate texts of all these addresses have been published in the Heidegger Collected Edition,[13] supplemented by the rewritten version that Heidegger composed at Pentecost-time in 1940, which is virtually identical with the first published edition (1943), though lacking chapter divisions and with different paragraphing. Thus, the student now has six chronologically distinct versions of Heidegger's work – three from 1930 and three from the 1940s. In addition, the German editor has provided appendices that indicate how Heidegger revised the Freiburg version in 1932, as he prepared it for an audience in Dresden, and revised it again in 1934; the editor has also provided footnotes to the various versions that record Heidegger's own marginalia. Realizing that Heidegger worked on this text for nineteen years, we can now follow its slow germination.

The 1930 addresses have great significance for us in studying other works of Heidegger from the 1930s: we now have the appropriate background material. Heidegger continued to probe the question of the essence of truth during the 1930s. He offered lecture courses under that very title, courses that have been published and translated fairly recently, one from 1931–32, *The Essence of Truth: On Plato's Parable of the Cave and the Theaetetus,*[14] another from 1933–34, *On the Essence of Truth.*[15] One offshoot of those courses was the essay "Plato's Doctrine of Truth."[16] Though that essay first appeared in print in 1942, it was often ascribed by earlier critics to the early 1930s because the university lectures on which it was based were not available. Here we can follow the trajectory from 1930 to 1942.

Heidegger's university lectures, published posthumously in Division II of his edition, *GA* volumes 17–63: Academic Lectures 1919–1944, frequently add clarification and detail to supplement the published works, and with respect to our topic of truth, the lectures make a considerable contribution. The two versions of the lecture course on Plato, **31–32** and **33–34**, borrowed their titles from our primary source and followed in the main the outline of argument that the address established, adding supplementary material for elucidation. Lectures resemble publications in that they were prepared for an academic audience, in this case a student audience that was decidedly discriminating and demanding. The lectures were mostly written out by Heidegger, and he planned their eventual publication; they were lucid in style, written for an oral delivery to be comprehended in a one-time hearing; they stand to his publications as an exposition does to a text.

We also cannot fail to note, in Division III of Heidegger's Works: Unpublished Manuscripts, the *Contributions to Philosophy,* which has a large section in the middle titled "The Essence of Truth."[17] This text is the earliest and fullest document of Heidegger's thinking in the period from 1936 onwards. In taking into account the further progressions of his thinking in the years of the 1930s, we can take guidance from the full-length study of *WW* that von Herrmann has published.[18] *WW* is, according to von Herrmann, the central text in the transition from Heidegger's early phenomenological philosophy to the later position that is described as *seinsgeschichtliches Denken* (understood literally, "thinking according to the history of being."). We shall have opportunity to document the interaction of *WW* with *GA* 65. Von Herrmann's reading[19] shows that in *WW,* the first step was taken from a fundamental ontology into *seinsgeschichtliches Denken,* in executing a curve from its earlier pages where "the essence of truth is freedom," to later pages, where the essence of freedom is shown to derive from concealment, the primordial essence of truth. And indeed we can document this very point, in part, even in the early texts of 1930. But, von Herrmann argues, a final step was not yet taken in any version of *WW* that would show how the exister's projective freedom is evoked (*ereignet*) through the withdrawal of being. This elucidates one decisive stretch along the course of Heidegger's *Denkweg*, his path of thinking, and it will help guide us in highlighting more detailed differences between drafts of *WW*.

In the broadest sense, Heidegger's *Denkweg* was the entire pathway from his beginnings (he was immersed in neo-scholasticism before he was exposed to neo-Kantianism) to the final seminars he offered in the 1970s.[20] For our present purpose, which focuses on the essence of truth, we can establish the main termini of this pathway as the latest of the three versions in each case: the terminus a quo being the Freiburg address of December 1930 and the terminus ad quem the published final text of 1949. Our study treats the former in Part I and the latter in Part II.

In juxtaposing the Freiburg 1930 address with the text of 1949, there is a balance to be struck between continuity and change.

(a) We recognize them as versions of the *same work*. The introduction to Part I will sketch the common character of all the versions, showing it to be a journey of thought that takes its start from a common experience of truth but undergoes a definite sequence of upheavals, to terminate in a final interrogation of essence. This pattern holds throughout and establishes the identity of this work in all versions. Heidegger himself commented in a note of 1940 that the questioning undertaken in the different versions had "maintained the same line of attack, the same basic views, and the same outline throughout."[21] Part I will make a few passing references in square brackets to the 1949 text at points where the latter supplements it without drastic revisions.

(b) But there are occasions where 1949 goes far beyond 1930 in ways that require separate treatment. That is the subject of Part II of this book. As we quoted from von Hermann above, *WW* is certainly in the course of surpassing the project of fundamental ontology, but we shall also note that it has not emancipated itself fully from fundamental ontology. It assigns a role to *Da-sein* in the constitution of truth that tends to obscure the main thrust of the argument. Thus, in the third unit of Part I, on Section I(b) of the address, we find the human being engaging in intending the objects of perception, anticipating the appearance of objects, setting itself to be bound by those objects. On the one hand, this makes the address relatively easy to follow. But on the other, it seems there remains a "humanistic" character of the account, with a role for human intentions in the constitution of truth, that would not finally content Heidegger. In the 1949 version (indeed also in 1940 and 1943) he introduced

> several other structures and forces into the account of experience, such as The Open and The Interval; these will be treated in Part II, Units 2 to 5 – an essential supplement to the earlier treatment, though not by any means a repudiation of it.

In this way, the early and late versions of *WW* exemplify the entire earlier and later thought of Heidegger, and it would be quite mistaken to suppose that the early versions were merely imperfect drafts of the work, destined to be discarded. In my view, the early versions – like Heidegger's early philosophy generally – assign a place to human projections and existence that is more readily intelligible *to us, to the reader*, than the final treatment, which is more austere. The reader who moves on to the later Heidegger after the early Heidegger should not feel a need to abandon the early work.

Nevertheless, Part II will show that the account of unconcealedness, *alētheia*, presented in 1930 as the essence of truth, needed to be modified though a wealth of historical mutations, expressed in ancient Greek and medieval and modern thought. Again, this does not *remove* unconcealedness as the essence of truth, but it does enshroud it.

Again, in Units 8 and 9 of Part I, we see Heidegger attempting to bring concealment into an essential relationship to unconcealment. Though he recognizes that concealment has not been produced by the human subject, he has not fully succeeded in finding an alternative account. But throughout the 1930s he will work out the doctrine of the *Ereignis*, and this will be evoked in the 1949 account of concealment, which we treat in Part II.

As a further point, I shall be showing at the end of Part I what the 1930 account of the essence of truth implied about the essence of knowledge and about the many disciplines by which we attain knowledge, and therefore about the university that affords the housing for philosophy and all the other disciplines. So we shall treat Heidegger's 1933 address on the German university as one outcome of the 1930 address. But in Part II we see that, as Heidegger grants more scope to concealment and mystery within the essence of truth, he must back away from his earlier claims about the right of philosophy to guide and rule other disciplines. This is closely tied to Heidegger's unfortunate political commitment in 1933 to the National Socialists. We give a brief account of this in the Intermission.

In a short monograph, *Die Kehre*,[22] Fräntzki has argued that the original draft of 1930 was not improved by the changes Heidegger introduced in the version finally published, which fell back into a kind of metaphysics that privileged unconcealment over concealment. I shall consider some of his arguments in the course of Part II.

PART I

The Early Pathway of Thinking

Freiburg, December 1930

Much of what Heidegger wrote in the years after *SZ* manifests the texture I call visible questioning, where the shape of the text is determined by questions written in the text. The practice of questioning invites the reader to accompany the author in the discovery of what can be put in question. Such questions are not intended as mere exercises for the mind – they proceed with serious concentration to offer answers. The questions are not rhetorical, as if he were withholding from the reader answers that he himself possessed. Rather, a reader who is willing to ask the questions seriously will then be inducted into a pathway of discovering answers. To be able to ask a question is an important achievement.

All of this is very true of the 1930 text, whose questions come close to outnumbering its assertions. Heidegger formulates his main question in words that we must not pass over carelessly: **Our topic is the *essence* of truth (*Wesen der Wahrheit*).**[23] This presupposes some initial acquaintance with truth, that is, with the phenomenon; and it divides the phenomenon from what is sought by the questioning: the essence. The question of the essence initiates a new kind of thinking that entails a complex interaction of questioning and answering, and we need to understand his term *Wesen*, essence, as tied to the practice of questioning – the term is inherently interrogative. There will be an initial appearance of essence where the thinking is relatively superficial, accomplished here in Section 1(a). Then, as the thinking proceeds, becoming deeper and more comprehensive, we find further, more complex versions of essence, *Wesen*, and the thinking practised in the essay is led to establish connections among them. Though the thinking begins from the usual concept of truth, the exposure to the *essence* of truth brings with it a series of upheavals in the thinking. The experience of thinking the essence of truth overcomes the habit of supposing there is a univocal concept of truth.

It is vital to grasp the internal arrangement of the address and of the essay in either version of the 1940s.[24] The text is not articulated as a single logical argument, establishing certain premises and drawing forth conclusions, and it is not unified as a set of doctrines about truth. Its unity is that of a pathway of thinking. The order of exposition is determined by the questions raised. An interlinked series of questions form an order of a different kind from a sequence of logical inferences. The answers to such questions are not related deductively to one another, because it is the intervening questions that constitute their order or sequence. Part I will trace the outline of the pathway by following the course of the 1930 address, which, being simpler than the published versions, lets the form of the outline appear clearly – the published *WW* also follows this plan, while adding certain elaborations to it. There is an intimate, narrower sense of the term *Denkweg* that is decisive for Heidegger and for my exposition: the course of a thinking offered *within* a single address or essay. The task of Part I will be to think along this micro-*Denkweg*.

As in the everyday use of the word "pathway," so here it must be understood to mean the direction of movement that has been imposed upon travellers in a given territory by the most prominent aspects of the territory itself. Attention to the pathway of thinking has to be accompanied by attention to the subject matter of thinking. That will be the structure of the essence in question: the essence of truth. Through giving close attention in thought to each particular phenomenon, we shall be led to the next one, and then the next. And as you move on from the starting point, you encounter several distinct phenomena that are given the name of truth (*die Wahrheit*). The later developments do not simply *displace* the topic of truth. If several distinct phenomena share the common name of "truth," Heidegger's essay will establish or reveal their connections, and what connects them all is what he calls "the essence of truth."

Only because the thinking starts off in a certain direction can it encounter that which forces it to bend, so that each arc is delineated by a thinking that is already under way, like a bird on the wing. I have introduced the term "Corners" to indicate the changes of direction that thinking must negotiate as it follows its subject, and attempt to show the reasons for the curving pathway, for the steps our thinking makes into such heterogeneous topics.[25]

Both the address and the essay are structured in three great movements, which might be described as three *Arcs* of thinking.

The First Arc

After the Introduction, the 1930 address unfolds in five sub-sections, while the 1949 text is articulated into nine chapters – but the two are of comparable length (about twenty pages) and, crucially, follow an identical outline, a pathway of questioning. The first lap in the journey overall moves through the first three layers or strata that belong to the essence of anything: I(a), what something *is*; and here we identify truth as the accordance of a statement with a thing; then, in I(b), we determine how it is *possible;* and in I(c). what gives *grounding* to that possibility. To complete this is the first Arc. Attached to the opening of the 1949 essay is a footnote that indicates, under (1), the initial sense of "essence." The first sense is the quiddity, which refers to a course of questioning, "What is truth? *Quid est veritas?*" But other layers or strata belong to the essence of anything. They constitute, as von Hermann expresses it,[26] the *Wesensgefälle* of truth, the ordering of strata within the essence. A fuller explanation will be found in Unit 4 of Part I.

Later units will acquaint us with other aspects of an essence. When Heidegger undertakes, in I(b), to explain how it is that statements actually do come to accord with, or correspond with, things, he is able to take this turn because of the conception of essence that is guiding him. It is a *corner* in the pathway of thinking to bring in this doctrine of essence. Moreover, there is a further *corner* accomplished in I(b), where Heidegger draws the conclusion that the possibility of truth is given by human conduct or comportment. Truth does not have its primary home in the statement. I(c) introduces a further *corner* in the pathway of thinking. With a very compressed argument that I shall attempt to unravel, Heidegger draws an interim conclusion from the phenomenology: the essence of truth is freedom. Here again, he redefines the concept of essence, as we shall see.

The Second Arc

The questioning cannot stop at I(c) however, and we turn another major *corner* at the beginning of II, introducing a second arc. We find that the essence of freedom is something utterly unexpected (what Heidegger calls "letting-be"), and then there are further movements and corners in Section II: we discover the ancient experience of unconcealedness, *alētheia,* as the historical essence of truth.

It is in this Second Arc that we encounter many of the most characteristic of Heidegger's philosophical preoccupations:

- *Existence.* The term *Existenz,* which was introduced on page 12 of *SZ,* was understood throughout the book to imply our reaching–out, our being opened up as being-in-the-world, our extension into a future about which we care, ontological structures that became interpreted through our special temporality. In *WW,* he frequently spells the word "Ek-sistenz," recalling its Greek root meaning "standing-out," though in 1930 he uses the Latin variant, *exsistence*. Thus our mode of being is distinct from the mode of being of other creatures, and of the objects in our environment that he characterizes with such terms as "readiness-to-hand" and "presence-at-hand."

- *Das Da-sein.* Closely connected with the doctrine of existence in *SZ* is Heidegger's idiosyncratic use of the term *Da-sein* to refer to ourselves; we shall take the occasion in Part I, Unit 7, and Part II, Unit 6, to treat the differences between his earlier and later use of this term.
- *Being. SZ* of course undertook the study of *Da-sein* (ourselves) with a further agenda in mind – Heidegger wanted to uncover the being of *Da-sein* (*das Sein des Da-seins*) with a view to opening up all the further reaches of the question of being – in part, by analysing that understanding of being that pertains to our being (*das vorontologische Seinsverständnis*). That kind of fundamental ontology is not repeated in the present essay on the essence of truth. Rather, what we experience is called, in this essay, beings as such, or beings as a whole (*das Seiende als solches und im Ganzen*). Just how the investigation of truth opens out upon beings, and their being, will concern us throughout the book.
- *Fate.* If at points Heidegger is referring to "modern" theories of truth, and also bringing forward the "ancient" experience of truth as unconcealedness, this might be seen as adding a historical dimension to his analysis of truth. But we cannot define this whole study as a "systematic" study that would then receive an "historical" supplement. The entire study moves in the dimension of history, which Heidegger conceives as *Geschichte*, which essentially includes ourselves in our contemporary thinking. We experience the *Geschick*, fate, of truth in modernity (Part II, Units 1, 7–11).

The Third Arc

At II(b) there looms up the most dangerous corner in the essence, where it must reach out to incorporate the Non-essence of truth (or, equivalently, the essence of untruth), the first form of which is concealment, executing a third arc. Probing it leads around a further corner to the untruth characteristic of human beings, erring, the final arc of thought. Of course, the question must arise with these intrusions of untruth: have we lost hold of truth itself, the *alētheia* we discovered just before? Truth is no longer merely adequation, no longer correctness, but now in the form of the primordial and ancient embodiment of truth – the unconcealedness of beings, and behind that the further unconcealedness of being. Thinking is thereby led into a deeper abyss where truth undergoes transformation into untruth, and that in two different forms, concealment and erring.

In Part II, our attention turns to the work that Heidegger undertook between the first conception of his essay and its publication, 1943 and 1949. The outline of the published essay remained the same, with the three main arcs still visible – the first in chapters 1–3, the second in chapter 4, and the third in chapters 5–7 – with the same corners turned in every arc. Part II, in earlier units, turns to the major revisions that appear in the 1943 and 1949 versions, which introduce several conditions for truth that go beyond the intentions and conduct of the individual.

1. Heidegger's Introduction: Questioning and the Public
(1930, pp. 379–81)

Our first foray into Heidegger's text treats his Introduction. He begins, as we would expect of a philosopher, by discriminating his question, What truth is, from the vast array of substantive inquiries, in economics, science, and so on, that seek to determine what is *the* truth in some particular sector of life (commerce, the material world, etc.). He is resolute in defending his philosophical question against attacks – stemming, he says, from "common sense" – that disparage purely abstract thinking. His challenge to the non-philosopher is: Can you express what you mean by "true"? [The text of the 1949 Introduction differs in only a few phrases.]

> **This is a treatment of the essence of truth, of that which makes every truth as such into a truth. In the question about the essence of truth, we do not trouble ourselves whether truth pertains to the practical experience of life or to economic calculation or technical considerations or skill in politics or scientific research or artistic creation. Looking away from all that, we are asking: what is truth altogether?** (pp. 379–80)

We are not to inquire into "the truth of the practical experience of life," nor the other cases: a truth gained through economic calculation, and so on. Thus the introductory paragraph circumscribes our question by contrasts. Far from denying that truth can be found through all these means, Heidegger is assuming that it can be, though their questions will not concern the present study. He avoids being distracted by questions about all these disciplines. Though the address thus gains in clarity, there will be another price paid, which we shall treat in detail after our survey in Part I. In 1933, when he was installed as rector of the university, he used his office to attempt a reform of the university, seeking to introduce a philosophical kind of questioning into all the faculties and disciplines of the university. Philosophy studies the essence of truth, and the lesser disciplines need to heed that and apply it in their efforts to establish the "truths" of nature and society. Yet it became apparent that the philosopher was not able to grasp what was specific to truth in each of these disciplines, so his initiative was unpopular and came to nothing. In later pages of Part II, we shall see how Heidegger later came to rethink the relation of philosophy to other disciplines

Often we call something that is true *a* truth (*eine Wahrheit*); no such "truths" are our quarry here, but rather truth itself (*die Wahrheit*), the one thing that distinguishes every "truth" as truth. If something true (e.g., in arithmetic) is called a "truth," the scare quotes cannot be omitted. In his main text, we shall not find the expression "a truth" any more: the noun "truth" from now on will be used only to signify what constitutes or distinguishes something that is true. He will emphasize this at the opening of Section I(a):

> **What do we usually understand by "truth"? Truth must be whatever makes a true thing true.** (p. 381)

Thus, in an elementary sense, "truth" is already a term of essence, namely the universal character common to everything true, but Heidegger does not consider this elementary grammatical distinction a genuine case of essence. Section I of the address treats the difference between something that is true, *the* truth, on the one hand, and the essence of truth, on the other; then it shows how they are connected.

In the Introduction, we read of a different form of *the* truth: an ideological claim of a partisan enthusiast who wishes to proclaim to us the *real* truth. But this too is different from the essence of truth. The second paragraph introduces an antagonist whose critical challenge drives the inquiry forward. He says: surely this question about the essence of truth exhibits exactly what is mistaken and useless about philosophy! Philosophy mounts up too high, where the air is too thin. Instead, he says, we should remain down on the ground, with the actual truth or the real truth (*die wirkliche Wahrheit*) by contrast with the abstract question. He is making a polarization, but it is not the same as the one the philosopher introduced at the beginning. There it was the one essence versus the many "truths," but now the antagonist is setting something singular, the actual or real truth, against the abstract essence of truth:

> **If our questioning had some genuine roots [*wurzelhaft*], and was prepared to take reality seriously, would it not first of all and last of all and without**

> **wavering be asking this: what is the real truth that can help us today when we are so oppressed by the events of the day, and give us security in the midst of the confusion of opinions?** (p. 380)

Though this critic is impatient with the philosopher's question, he does not seem to be a dogmatist – he does not claim to possess the real truth, but rather is insisting that the real truth is what we need urgently to *find*: perhaps there will be a real prophet who will come to resolve our confusions and divisions. The antagonist wants a radical (*wurzelhaftes*) thinking, turned to what is actual, and he has an expectation of guidance from a political source. There were powerful currents of radical political thinking current in Heidegger's time, and here he recognizes their demands while distancing his philosophical question from them. This recognition is something new in Heidegger. One cannot miss the pathos, in the Germany of the 1930s, of this appeal that we read just above.

The denigration of philosophy that we are finding here recalls Plato's portraits of the antagonists of Socrates. In the *Gorgias* 484 c–486 c, the lawyer Callicles mocks the idealism of Socrates's questioning about justice: philosophy makes one unfit, unequipped for the serious business of struggle, competition, courts, and money-making. Yet even after that critique, it was still possible for Socrates, at *Gorgias* 488 b, to resume his questioning to Callicles: what then does he consider justice to be? That is a general question, and it can still be asked because when Callicles mocked Socrates's inquiries into justice, he did not repudiate justice completely but promoted his doctrine about natural and conventional justice. That gave Socrates his leverage. And similarly, Heidegger's antagonist still holds to his real, actual "truth." Thus we can see that the very first movement of thought in *WW* mounts up to the essence in a manner reminiscent of Plato. This Platonic starting point will have reverberation right to the end of the address.

Heidegger acknowledges that the critic's view has its reasons and that the philosopher too must share an interest in what is real. He defines the viewpoint of the antagonist as common sense, *gesunder Menschenverstand*, constitutionally and permanently inimical to philosophy. Even though common sense is the permanent antagonist of philosophy, the philosopher too acknowledges that he is imbued through and through with common sense, so the dialogue that we are studying is actually taking place inside the philosopher. Heidegger even says that there can be no refutation of common sense by philosophy. We wonder then whether there can be no reply at all to the promptings of common sense, whether the philosopher is in a hopeless position: our text says that the attack only brings to light the situation to which philosophizing has always found itself relegated. Heidegger shows the way forward, continuing the dialogue with a line of *questioning*. The antagonist may have dismissed the philosophical question on the essence of truth, but not truth itself, so it is suitable to pose to him the question after all, what, then, he means by "truth."

> **We were being urged to ask for the real truth and express it! They want us to answer the question where we stand today. They want to know the real truth: how things stand with us today. The real truth! So it is truth they want! In calling for the real truth, they presumably know already what one means in general by truth. Or do they only have a sort of feeling for that, know it only in a general way, only approximately – i.e., basically not at all, and certainly not with appropriate knowledge?** (p. 381)

From his education through his early teaching years, and his great success with *SZ*, Heidegger had been a very academic philosopher, working on epistemology, metaphysics, and logic with a lot of attention to antiquity and the Middle Ages. Now he is stepping out into the bright light of the public arena and engaging in combat. The radical currents of the 1920s were often Marxist, expressing what we see in the *Theses on Feuerbach*, of which the second reads:

> The question whether objective truth can be attributed to human thinking is not a question of theory but is a practical question. In practice man must prove the truth, that is, the reality and power, the this-sidedness of his thinking. The dispute over the reality or non-reality of thinking which is isolated from practice is a purely scholastic question.[27]

An antagonism towards philosophy was often expressed by the Left in Weimar Germany, where Marxist parties believed they could offer leadership. All the writings and activism of Lenin, so powerful in Germany in the 1920s, exemplify a realism and radicalism that met this standard. Always scornful of philosophical idealism, Lenin insisted on the "correctness of the political leadership exercised by [the Bolsheviks]; … their political strategy and tactics" were confirmed to the "broad masses, who have seen from their own experience that they are correct."[28] The radical realism that the antagonist is calling for was not only on offer from the Left in those days. It was available from the Right as well. In an article he published in the journal he edited, *Avanti!*, October 1914, Benito Mussolini attacked the abstractions of idealism, precisely at the time he was abandoning the pacifism and internationalism of the Socialists for the *Fasci*:

> A party which wishes to live in history and ... to make history, cannot submit ... to a line which is dependent on an unarguable dogma or an eternal law, separate from the iron necessity of change over space and time ... We have the privilege of living at the most tragic hour in world history. Do we ... want to be inert spectators of this huge drama? Or do we want to be ... the protagonists?[29]

In taking on the Left and the Right here, Heidegger has definitely come down from his ivory tower. But he did not long sustain this stout posture of the philosopher's independence – in the coming year, 1931, Martin and Elfride Heidegger could be heard defending the policies of the National Socialists in Germany. This opinion did not originate in Heidegger's philosophical work – it arose out of their appraisal of Germany's economic situation. Nevertheless, it did come to affect Heidegger's academic work up to 1933 and 1934, and entered into his writings for those two years, with considerable damage to his reputation.

By 1928, Heidegger had left Marburg University to take up an appointment as Ordinarius for Philosophy in Freiburg as the successor to Husserl, who was retiring. At the reception for Husserl in April 1928, Heidegger spoke for all the phenomenological scholars, and presented Husserl with a festschrift that included his own essay "On the Essence of Ground." At his formal installation in July 1929, Heidegger delivered the address "What Is Metaphysics? (*WM*)" to an audience embracing most of the university, and this was followed by the lecture course "The Fundamental Concepts of Metaphysics" (*GA* 29–30), which seemed to aim at a comprehensive philosophical orientation, less technically phenomenological than his previous work. It was not long after this that he offered his address *WW* at several universities, including Freiburg in December 1930.

WM has a programmatic thrust that bears on university studies in general Especially he stresses the separation, even alienation, of academic fields from one another, and this provides the opportunity to introduce to his audience the place of philosophy – now identified as metaphysics – relative to all other disciplines and faculties. The philosopher first affirms his solidarity with the whole academic project:

> **Our existence – in the community of researchers, teachers and students – is determined by *Wissenschaft*.**[30]

Then he opens up a place for philosophy by determining its vocation:

> **The scientific fields are quite diverse. The ways they treat their objects of inquiry differ fundamentally. Today only the technical organization**

> **of universities and faculties consolidates this multiplicity of dispersed disciplines; the practical establishment of goals by each discipline provides the only meaningful source of unity. Nonetheless, the rootedness of the sciences in their essential ground has atrophied.**[31]

The next sentence points the way to the vocation of philosophy:

> **[I]n all the sciences we adopt a stance towards beings themselves.**

The bulk of the address then raises the question concerning being by way of a special examination of the Nothing, *das Nichts.* The end of the address establishes that it is through metaphysics – in exploring being and the Nothing – that we encounter the hidden and unitary grounding for all disciplines:

> **Only if science exists on the basis of metaphysics can it fulfill in ever-renewed ways its essential task, which is not to amass and classify bits of knowledge, but to disclose in ever-renewed fashion the entire expanse of truth in nature and history.**[32]

In later decades Heidegger was to quote again and again these words from 1929 that cleared the way for the vocation of philosophy: we find them in his 1945 Memorandum "The Rectorate 1933–34: Facts and Thoughts," paragraph 2[33]; and they are prominently quoted in the interview that the *Spiegel* published in 1976: "Only a God Can Save Us."[34] Not surprisingly, in view of our last quotation above, Heidegger's later references connect the question of the grounding of the different disciplines to the question of *truth,* specifically to the *essence* of truth; in this way he was able to connect *WW* to *WM,* the two of them only a year apart:

> **The university had to renew itself out of the ground of its own essence, i.e., the grounding for the essence of the sciences, namely out of the essence of truth itself.** [35]

Thereby the university would restore the original living unity of its scholars.

A short address like *WM* could hardly develop in detail just how the grounding of knowledge – the essence of truth – was connected to concrete researches in mathematics, chemistry, physics, biology; in law, medicine, and pedagogy; in theology, literature, and the historical sciences. In this respect, it reminds us of the opening paragraph of *WW,* which, as we noted at the start, marked off the philosophical question from the "truths" of economics, politics, scientific research, and art without addressing any questions about them as particular occasions of truth. The outline of the problem is shown at the end of *WM*:

> **Only because the Nothing is manifest can science make beings themselves objects of investigation.**[36]

We need to ask just why that is so. How could mathematical studies, for instance, depend upon our exposure to the Nothing? Or, for that matter, exposure to the question of being? And in what way is truth in mathematics dependent upon the essence of truth? Heidegger's talk committed him to investigate such questions. (See the Intermission below.)

2. Accordance of Statement and Thing: Section I(a) *(1930, pp. 381–3)*

Now, with the help of modern and medieval philosophers, we entertain the concept of truth as agreement or accordance. Section I(a) clarifies what belongs to this concept, and later parts of Section I explore how accordance is possible – the first lap in the journey overall. It is not by assembling data from everyday speech that Heidegger arrives at the concept; it draws on the work of earlier philosophers. *SZ* 44 had already cited the majority of contemporary philosophers who espoused such a view, though here Heidegger drafts it in a new format. We are pointed away from the messy details of ordinary language, towards the domain of *concepts*, where there is the clarity of a duality: the concept "truth," *die Wahrheit*, stands over against this instance or that, something true, *ein Wahres*, and it is what governs the instances, is responsible for their truth, makes them true.

Essence is to be understood initially in the sense of quiddity, the "What." We can look at the place of quiddity in philosophy in general in the *Basic Problems of Phenomenology* (1927),[37] Section 10(b), which, though addressed to medieval scholastic philosophy, can also highlight Heidegger's own use of the term for us. In the scholastic scheme, something becomes actual only after its nature or *quidditas* has been determined. This is also anticipated in Aristotle, who formulates *what* something is (*ti estin*) as what it has already been (*to ti ēn einai, quod quid erat esse*). These past tenses do not signify past time exactly, but rather what was primordial: what something *is* must come first, before anything else can be established about a subject, and that is the essence: what something had been all along. *Wesen ist, was gewesen ist.* We are beginning with the idea that there is such an essence and that it can be found and expressed in words.

Now to apply the point to truth. If there is something true, *p*, then the essence of truth is what must have been decided beforehand, must have held in advance for *p*, if it is to be granted a place among the "truths." If you have been wondering whether *p* is true, you might then ask further in a philosophical spirit, "What is truth?" You'd want that answer to find application to the statement *p* from which you started, and to every true statement. This initial step offers no data concerning what truth *is*. It merely has the force of directing us into the form of conceptual thinking, which philosophical study requires. Now Heidegger can take the next step forward, for the class of instances can be divided into two. What is true, *ein Wahres*, can be a thing, *eine Sache*, or a statement, *eine Aussage.*

> **(a) What then can be true? We say, for instance, that it is a true delight to work together with this person or that one. We mean that it is a pure delight, a real delight. The true is the real. Accordingly we speak of true gold in contrast with the false. False gold is not really what it appears to be – it is mere semblance, the unreal as opposed to the real, the true.** (p. 381)

We experience here a reversal over against the Introduction's debate between the philosopher and the antagonist. There we saw an opposition between the true and the real; the antagonist insisted on dealing with reality, *das Wirkliche, die Wirklichkeit,* and resisted inquiring into truth's essence. Yet now that precise opposition vanishes: it seems that the true *is* the real! (Here we must note that Heidegger's term *wirklich* could also be translated as "actual, actuality," as in Sallis's translation of *WW* 1949.)

Heidegger notes an important qualification. In another sense, things that are not true in this way can nonetheless be said to be real. If something stands exposed as fraudulent or false gold, it is nevertheless something real, in another sense of the term, because we see it and grasp it as surely as we do the real gold. Why is there this apparent difference between the expressions? Why is it that when something seemingly goldlike fails to be true gold, and fails to be real gold, it is nonetheless still said to be real? There is a double meaning of "real" (or "actual"), an equivocation. The true is, as it were, only one half of the real when the false thing is also real. But there is no equivocation in the term "true:" it is used to discriminate genuine gold from the fake. The true gold is called *genuine (echt).* We express this in English with the adverb "truly" – "It's truly gold" or "It's not truly gold" – and we use the adverbs "really" and "actually" to express this same point – "It's not really gold, it's not actually gold," since the adverbs are not subject to the equivocation that we noticed.

If we ask now what "true" means we have this lead: we say of the true gold or genuine gold that *es stimmt*, "it's in accord." The case of a true thing, and its contrast with the spurious or the fake, depends on a criterion by which the thing is measured, a standard defined in advance: what we understand gold to be. The verb *stimmen* will appear in many combinations in these pages, but the simple root verb appears here first of all as the normal way of expressing a suspicion, when we are just beginning to surmise a deception – "something is not quite right here," *hier stimmt etwas nicht* – that is, this looks like a counterfeit. It is against this background experience of *nicht-stimmen* that we are able to confirm the positive case of agreement, when we say "It's all right," *es stimmt.* Heidegger understands *stimmen* both to signify approval and to signify agreement: the thing is in accord with what it ought to be. He will go on next to the case of a statement's being true, and the rest of the address will deal with that, leaving the truth of things behind, but the mention of true delight and true gold has the function of introducing *stimmen* as central to truth.

We turn next to the other branch (b) of what is true: statements, *Aussagen*, propositions and cognitions, *Sätze und Erkenntnisse.* This change of subject remains in force for the whole of the essay. A statement is true not merely by agreeing, *einstimmen*, but by corresponding, if

> **what it means and says corresponds [*übereinstimmt*] with the matter about which the statement is made.** (p. 382)

A true statement is not grasped merely as a real or actual statement, contrasted with a fake one or a spurious one, that is, one that does not fully succeed in being a statement, for example, owing to confused speech. Rather, it is contrasted with one that is false, which is something quite different. Still, Heidegger recognizes the common core shared with the previous cases, for he is ready to say of the true statement that *es stimmt*:

> **Here too we say that it is in accord [*es stimmt*]. But here it is not the object that is in accord, but the statement, the proposition.** (p. 382)

The rest of the text will be devoted to explaining what that means and how it is possible. Up to here we have laid out two parallel cases:

> **Whatever is true, be it a real thing that is true or a true proposition, is that which accords, that which is in accordance. Being true, truth, means accordance. And that in a twofold way: first the agreement of a thing with what is intended in advance about it, and then the correspondence of what is intended in the statement to the thing. This double character of**

> **the according is expressed in the traditional definition of truth: *veritas est adaequatio rei et intellectus.*** (p. 382)

This conclusion will stand throughout the remainder of the text. That is all implied in what Heidegger calls "the traditional definition of truth": truth is the adequation of the thing and the intellect, realized in the simultaneity of the agreements running in two directions.

Heidegger introduces the Scholastic Latin term *adaequatio rei et intellectus* to echo his own terms *stimmen* (in English rendered as "accord"), and *übereinstimmen* of statement and thing. In *SZ*, Section 44(a), he attributed the Latin phrase *adaequatio intellectus et rei* to Aquinas's *Quaestiones disputatae de veritate.*[38] Here a preliminary word on terminology. We can use the English word "adequation" to render Heidegger's *Angleichung*, because it is Heidegger's rendering of Aquinas's *adaequatio.* But there is nothing wrong with rendering it "correspondence" either; there is no essential problem of terminology here. Heidegger is exploring the adequation or correspondence (*Angleichung*) that produces accordance (*stimmen*), and either one of these can be regarded as the quiddity of truth. At this stage in our pathway, we need to recognize that the Latin terms are the authoritative ones, and if we provide the Latin word to back up the English or German versions, there will be no confusion. This has all been passed down in our inherited language. So we have given an account of the common meaning of the word, together with an account of the traditional metaphysical concept that defined it. Clearly the metaphysical tradition has helped determine the people's language.

A summary:

- *ueberEinstimmen* (used of statements) translated "correspond"
- *Einstimmen* (of things) translated "agree"
- *Stimmen* (generically applied to thing or statement) translated "accord"
- *Angleichung* (of statement or thing) translated "adequation"

Heidegger's account expresses ideas that had been current in philosophy for decades. Most likely, we can see its primary source in Husserl, originating as a revision and simplification of the account of truth Husserl offered in his *Logical Investigations.* In the 6th Investigation of the 2nd Part, he had defined truth through the interaction of our cognitive intentions and their fulfilment.[39] In particular Husserl offered four meanings of the concept of truth, of which the third was the being-true of an object or thing, corresponding to Heidegger's genuineness; the second was the traditional *adaequatio intellectus et rei*, Heidegger's *Übereinstimmung* of statement with thing. These accounts should be recognizable to philosophers in the analytic tradition who have studied "the correspondence theory of truth." The correspondence theory of truth was defended by Russell (among many others), for instance, in his William James lectures in 1940,[40] particularly where it applied to statements and beliefs, though Russell had nothing like the views of Husserl and Heidegger on truth in things.

We also need to take into account larger units of discourse and representation that may also be judged true or false. Modern philosophy, influenced by logic, has tended to put so much stress on the statement that its analyses have frequently occluded the larger units. But we must bear in mind narratives, especially in history, and treatises, especially in the sciences, whose truth would seem to be of a kind with the contemporary views we have been treating. The historical narrative is true if what it describes are events that really happened; the scientific treatise is true if the world actually is as it asserts. We can acknowledge this without needing to enter into the question of the Whole and Part: whether the truth of the whole is reducible to the truth of each of the atomic statements that make it up. That question, of course, was set aside by Heidegger at the opening of his Introduction to *WW*, when he set aside various questions as to what is true. We can also recognize the broader reach of truth beyond such academic cases. Historical novels and movies can be "based on real life" and thereby make a claim to truth of a different kind than historical research as such. Movies can be set in "the actual location." Those truth-claims are of a kind with the contemporary views we have been reviewing here.

Another matter now appears that seems to our common sense to be self-evident: that truth has an opposite, or that there is untruth. Truth has two opposites: semblance as the untruth of a thing and falsehood as the untruth of a statement. Heidegger says in all versions of his text that it is common for us to think that untruth, in either form, could be left aside in an inquiry into truth. Reference to the opposites might seem to constitute an innocent, harmless addition to the study. But in the sequence we shall learn that it is anything but that. An inquiry into *essence* cannot leave truth's opposites lying outside the essence.

Next Heidegger recognizes the unsatisfactory character of this newly defined essence or definition of truth:

> **Thereby the first step has been taken in coming to know the essence. What we commonly understand by truth has been asserted. But this assertion of the common essence of truth offers so meagre an answer to the question of the essence that not only has it failed to bring a concluding answer, it has not even accomplished a beginning of the question.** (pp. 382–3)

These remarks pave the way for further studies to come in the pages that follow. The linguistic-conceptual explanation of truth falls short of our interest in the essence. Why is that? What more can we demand? Heidegger says that we have not yet even begun to question, that is, to think. We can understand that from the next Section, I(b): when we proceed to ask how the correspondence comes to prevail, yielding the truth of statements, our investigation will actually uncover how a statement is even possible in the first place. First, we shall need to *characterize* correspondence. And then, more than a clarification, Heidegger will be requiring in the next chapter that we also *explain* just how the statement *does* adapt itself to the thing, or come into concert with the thing, yielding truth.

As we anticipate the treatment to follow, we should not expect Heidegger to hold to all the basics of the scholastic approach to truth – in particular to assume that "true" is pre-eminently assigned to the statement or *intellectus.* Throughout the 1920s he grappled repeatedly with Aristotle in a way that detached Aristotle from the scholastic tradition, seeking to view his thought phenomenologically. The tradition tended to assume that it is in every case a statement (or sentence or proposition) that is true – it is the "truth-bearer." But that is what Heidegger submits to a critique, in a meditation motivated by Aristotle, in the *Logic* lectures of 1925–26 (*GA* 21).[41] Heidegger approaches logic as Aristotle had done in the *de Interpretatione,* first conceptualizing the statement (*Aussage*) as a *logos* that points something out (*apophantikos*) and then treating the possibility of its truth or falsity. But (*GA* 21, pp. 127–8) he is critical of the prevailing accounts of Aristotelian logic, especially the book on syllogisms by Maier that was at that time very influential,[42] which claimed that truth belonged properly to the statement or judgment, and that truth in perception or representing was a derivative and altered concept of truth. In a close reading of the *de Interpretatione,* Heidegger shows that Aristotle did not make truth depend on the statement: the statement is not the location of truth and falsity; that is, it is not the truth-bearer. Aristotle has shown, on the contrary, that (possible) truth and (possible) falsity are the home, or location, of the statement: *Satz ist nicht der Ort der Wahrheit, sondern Wahrheit der Ort des Satzes* (p. 135). This emerges from the words that Aristotle uses at 17 a 2–3: *apophantikos ou pas, all' en hō to alētheuein ē pseudesthai hyparchei,* which Heidegger understands (p. 129) to mean that what defines the statement is the possibility of being true or false; truth and falsity are not attributes of the statement, but vice versa.[43] A proper logical theory would put things in reverse: it would recognize that the true and the false are statement-bearers. This relationship can be comprehended by virtue of the special senses of the Greek words in the text. Aristotle's verb *alētheuein* means "uncovering, removing the concealment of something," and its contrary *pseudesthai* means "deceiving, covering up" (pp. 131–2). The operative term for the statement, *apophantikos, apophansis,* means "letting something be seen" (*aufweisen, sehen-lassen*). The true and the false are what make statements themselves possible. Only the discourse that uncovers or covers up achieves a letting-be-seen (the making of a statement).[44] Heidegger now goes further (as he will do in *SZ,* Section 33) in deriving from the apophantic character of the statement its further functions as predicating and communicating. But all this leads to the inescapable question: if truth is not defined with reference to the statement, how then is it to be grasped?

The main thing Heidegger has shown in this analysis is that truth and falsity are the presupposed, non-discursive grounding for statements themselves, which then become capable of being true or false in a secondary and derivative way. Taking the matter further in *SZ,* Heidegger shows that Aristotle never made the statement, *logos,* the primary occasion of truth, since sense-perception and understanding discovered truth without discourse, that is, without *logos.* In *SZ,* p. 33, we read that in the Aristotle texts, what is true, "indeed more originally true than the *logos,*" is the simple sense-perception of something, *aisthēsis* ("Looking always discovers colours, hearing always discovers tones"). Moreover, the non-discursive *nous* or *noein,* the purest, simplest exposure to what-is, is what is pre-eminently true.

In addition, to supplement the Aristotle exegesis, Heidegger offered many arguments of his own in various texts of the 1920s, for example, in *On the Essence of Ground,*[45] to show that we do experience a pre-predicative truth, that there is, prior to predication, a revealing that is not itself predicative.

Propositional truth is rooted in a more original truth (unconcealedness), in the pre-predicative manifestation of beings, "ontic truth."

I began the Introduction to this book with the claim that, for Heidegger, truth is the *medium* for all experience, with a reference to the Platonic analogy of light. What we have just rehearsed is a first instance of this idea.

3. Truth Prior to the Statement: Section I(b) *(1930, pp. 383–7)*

We may be surprised to note that Heidegger begins this section by proposing to let the thing-agreement drop out of sight: he follows the "traditional" path of philosophy in focusing on the truth of statements. As for the corresponding achieved by the statement, we need to ask not only what that *means* (*was heißt Übereinstimmen?*), but even more how it comes to pass ("how does it find a foothold? ... *seinen inneren Halt?*," p. 383). The fact that this question arises now reflects the guiding idea of "essence," introducing the second element after the quiddity, namely what makes truth possible. So we shall be turning a major *Corner* in the inquiry, moving to a deeper stratum of the essence of truth. The text has already acknowledged in Section I(a) that when the common use of the word "truth" and the common concept have been explained, we have not yet even begun to question, that is, to think.

What then, as a whole, is the argument of I(b)? Assuming the traditional quiddity – the statement's accordance – Heidegger will seek to derive the truth of statements from an account of our intending, *meinen*, the object of the statement. He will focus on our conduct, *Verhalten*, that plays a mediating role in forming our intending. That point then permits Heidegger to identify the salient feature that defines truth itself, the standard, *Mass*, that a thing presents to our conduct and that is inherited by the intending and the statement. This is the phenomenon of truth that is prior to the statement, as we anticipated at the conclusion of the preceding Unit 2. Excavating the truth-accordance brings to the fore this series of factors or elements that belong to truth and that will play a role in all the later paragraphs of the address.

The present question, then, in two parts, is stated on page 383:

> **We ask: what does it mean for a statement to correspond to a thing? What allows such corresponding to find a foothold [*seinen inneren Halt*]?**

The present question is looking for the "inner connection," "den inneren Halt," of statement and thing. And in calling it an "inner possibility," as in the penultimate paragraph of the Section, Heidegger is pointing us away from an external possibility, as when someone might chart correlations between statements and things, so that the statement "snow is white" would be in accordance just in case snow actually was white,[46] the mere statistical correlation. "Inner possibility" refers rather to something within the statement itself that makes accordance possible, but of course Heidegger does not mean here one of the *words* that the statement contains. He will show that it is our human conduct that is interior to the possibility of the statement.

The thinking in the earlier portion of the address and the essay is thoroughly phenomenological. Though Heidegger does not use that term here, we can see that it fits because he is engaging in a description of experience, not a mere analysis of concepts. In treating true statements, Heidegger does not see the speaker as detached from his milieu, and he does not speak of truth as carried by beliefs. The speaker is thrust forward into his milieu in close encounters. Heidegger's view of experience appears in this remark from the address:

> **Truth is no mere subjective occurrence in a proposition, but the revealing exposure to the revealed beings as such. All human conduct is revelatory in this way or that ...** (p. 394)

There are certainly many statements that are not forged in this kind of experience, not in the presence of the object, but are nevertheless true. Heidegger's phenomenology deals with what other philosophers have called observation statements. That Caesar was killed on the Ides of March is true even though none of us have experienced that. Such statements are true, but they do not manifest the *essence* of truth. Heidegger's thinking wants to take account of both kinds, those that show the essence and those that do not. Many statements of history, mathematics, and science are true but do not make the essence visible.

Heidegger's phenomenology intends to capture our *experience* – saying something true, hearing something and verifying it, or even a wordless perception. The statement interests us in its correlation with perception and action – the encounter in the living presence of a thing. He is scrutinizing the encounter between an articulate, speaking self and something that is being seen. Our investigation is to uncover how a statement is actually possible. A phenomenological account will treat experience as the wellspring of statements and by the same token the birthplace of truth. The statement as such originates from the same matrix as does truth. The analysis does not treat the statement as a neutral entity, either true or false. That would belong to a non-phenomenological form of thinking – phenomenology, rather, traces the origin of utterance to truth itself. Heidegger will turn to questions about falsity and other kinds of untruth only at a later point in the study. Heidegger is reaching down into the sub-structure of all experience that underlies all epistemological and linguistic theories. A statement not grounded in experience might after all be true – but it would not manifest the essence of truth.

We can see, from Heidegger's description of his examples, that the statement is based in the kind of experience he has already treated in *SZ*, everyday "circumspective concern." The situation involves a speaker addressing someone in the presence of a table on which some coins are lying. He is speaking of one of them (a five-mark coin), singling it out in some way, saying "*This* coin ..." The speaker's bearing or conduct or comportment (*Verhalten*) stands open to (*sich öffnet zu*) this five-mark coin, taking note of its attributes, colour, metallic composition, shape – it's called a *vorhanden* coin, though of course everyone understands it to be *zuhanden* too (i.e., of a definite value). All of these attributes give guidance to everyone's *alltägliches umsichtiges* interaction with the coin. Whether or not any words are spoken, their conduct is infused with discourse, *die Rede*, and they can all *see* that the coin is round.

The question of the inner possibility of accordance is posed for us by a comparison with the case of two things that have a correspondence (*Übereinstimmen*) with each other: two coins on the table that are both five-mark coins. Their correspondence is their being similar (*gleich*) in appearance (*Aussehen*), though Heidegger is also assuming further aspects – their equivalence in value, for example:

> **We speak of corresponding in different senses: we say, for example, with regard to two five-mark coins lying on the table: they correspond to one another. They are just like one another in the way they look. They have this in common, and they are in this respect the same as one another.** (p. 383)

This coin-correspondence is introduced only to sharpen a contrast with the correspondence that interests us, and raise our perplexity:

> **We also speak of corresponding when, for example, we make a statement about one of the five-mark coins there, "This coin is round." The statement corresponds with the thing.** (p. 384)

But we can find no similarity between statement and coin – Heidegger lists a series of contrasts confirming their dissimilarity (*Ungleichheit*). This raises the question particularly about the *type* of correspondence the theory of truth has specified: it is supposed to be an adequation (*Angleichung*), but we do not seem to find anything here that is *gleich*, and it doesn't become coin-like.

> **The statement must remain – indeed even first become – what it is.** (p. 384)

So if there is an adequation or correspondence, it must be defined through some factor proper to the statement that is missing in the case of the two similar coins. This relationship is called intending, *meinen*, in 1930 (but in the later versions is given the name *Vor-stellen*, presenting). The German word *meinen* is not *Intention*, that rather technical term of phenomenology:

> **The statement comes into connection with the five-mark coin in that it *meint* [the coin].** (p. 384)

The statement accomplishes a *meinen* in that something is being stated (the illocutionary content of the utterance), and this is something determinate, *Bestimmtes.* Making a statement about something is a *conduct* towards it (*Verhalten zu –*), and it is within the conduct that the adequation of the statement to the thing is accomplished. Crucially, that means that the conduct has responded to the thing by conducting itself

> **in just the way the thing requires of the conduct.** (Ibid.)

It is from this last point that the main inference is drawn: there is a directive, ***ein innerer Auftrag,*** to which the statement submits.

In this very semester 1930–31, Heidegger has been offering a lecture course on Hegel's *Phenomenology of Spirit*,[47] with detailed treatment of its first chapter, "Sense Certainty: The 'This' and *Meinen.*" Hegel used the term *meinen* for the immediate certainty that a sensuous consciousness has of a single "this," lacking any universal predicates, such as "coin" or "round" – it apprehended only the being of "this." Because this *meinen* excluded everything universal, it finds itself tripped up and refuted by language, which is full of universals (predicates, times and places, every "I" and "Thou"). It lacks truth. It cannot survive and is forced to undergo transformation into a different kind of consciousness, what Hegel called "Perception." But in his own scrutiny of this *meinen,* Heidegger cannot be confident of such an abstract object, a mere "this" deprived of every determinate predicate – that hypothesis depended on Hegel's project of dialectic which had to take its start from the most primitive and unpromising form of consciousness in order to proceed on its pilgrimage to spirit. Thus there is a *meinen,* according to Heidegger, that can intend "This coin is round." In the sub-section "Language and the expression of what is universal and the singular item which is intended," he agrees with Hegel that *meinen* intends always the "this" and that language is the corrective to the inarticulate sense-certainty;[48] but for Heidegger, language is present in all our experience and *meinen,* "which is not at all the case for Hegel."[49]. Heidegger's phenomenology does not accommodate the stage of sense-certainty: "this" is always "this table" or "this coin."

The statement gives utterance to a *meinen,* but this latter has its substratum in a conduct (*Verhalten*):

> **A statement is, in itself, a statement about something, and making a statement about something is a certain conduct towards that something, and the adequation of the statement to the thing is an adequation accomplished within that conduct. That means that the conduct towards something conducts itself towards it in just the way that this thing requires**

> **of such a conduct. This "just so" is the inner directive [*Auftrag*] to which the statement submits. The statement brings this directive along with it. But it is not that, in making a statement, one gives such a directive to oneself; rather, the directive is assigned to the statement-making insofar as it is a *conduct*. What is bestowed on the conduct as such is the inner directive to engage itself with that towards which it is conducting itself, and a directive regarding the manner of the conduct.** (pp. 384–5)

The conduct *makes itself open* (*Sich-Öffnen*) to the thing. With this term, we are coming close to the specific vocabulary of truth that this address will offer. The next line makes the link still tighter: since there is a *Sich-Öffnen*, we can say that every conduct is revelatory, *offenbart*:

> **Through this self-engagement, the conduct opens itself [*das Verhalten ist dabei ein sich-Öffnen*] for that towards which it conducts itself. And the self-engaging shows an openness towards the conduct too. Thus we say: every conduct reveals; nevertheless not every conduct is a making-manifest in the sense of identifying cognitively.** (pp. 384–5)

Because the *Verhalten* makes itself open, it can respond to a thing. What a coin requires of us is to pick it up, to pocket it, to spend it, to donate it, or to roll it: its relevance (*SZ: Bewandtnis*) is fully established in a social world. The appropriateness of response enters into the conduct: we use it in *Such* a way *As* (*So-Wie*) it would require of anyone: this is a directive that is called "inner," meaning that it informs and guides the conduct. *Auftrag* means command, commission, order, usually thought of as imposed by an authority, but here imposed by the humblest little thing, a coin. The conduct accomplishes an adequation to the thing by assimilating this directive imposed by the thing. The conduct is the *Such* – while the directive gives the *As* –. In the scene we are witnessing, however, it seems, nobody actually picks this coin up, or pockets it or rolls it; we find, rather, that just making a statement about it is already conduct enough. But conduct can be appropriate or inappropriate.

[This *Auftrag*, directive, undergoes a split in the revised essay of 1943 and 1949. In Part II, Unit 3, we see a difference between the specific standard, *Mass*, imposed by the thing, and the general directive, *Weisung*, that we ought to pay heed to that which shows itself, a directive that springs from our being-in-the-world.]

Not only is the conduct opened up – the thing in question, such as a coin, becomes revealed. Heidegger expends great effort on securing this point. Here there are several examples that are supposed to clarify both the self-opening and the revelatory power of conduct. The conduct of labour reveals the products and the entire productive process, contrasted with the external gaze of someone who merely looks on, an abstract exteriority that is here called cognitive and theoretical. Personal commitment to someone reveals the human being, not mere observation and psychology. It is within the conduct that the adequation of the statement to the thing is accomplished.

Can we grasp what it means to view a statement as a form of conduct? That is a question addressed in *SZ*, Section 33, "The Statement as a Derivative Mode of Interpretation." In Sections 31 and 32, Heidegger has treated our perceptions and actions as forms of understanding and interpreting the world, and here he derives the statement's accomplishments – predicating, communicating and pointing out (*apophansis*) – as deriving from practical involvements. In the course of construction work a carpenter might call out to his helper, "Too heavy! The other hammer!" Such practice-driven utterance is a base for the grammatically formed predicating statement "The hammer is heavy," revealing that conduct perseveres within statements, just as he treats it in the present 1930 text.

[Neither in *SZ* nor in the 1930 addresses did Heidegger undertake a complete and rigorous deduction of the statement from our everyday conduct. That is what we shall treat in Part II, Unit 3, devoted to *WW* (1949) with its account of *Vor-stellen* and its *Entgegen-stehen-lassen*, which incorporates the very form of a statement.]

We have been speaking about an inner directive, inner because it informs the conduct that is related to a thing. Heidegger wants to treat this more exactly, to focus on the standard, *Mass* (p. 386), that the thing sets for our conduct, which is also called a binding force, *Bindendes, Verbindendes*: the question is how a standard comes into play. The conduct accepts the binding force that is expressed in the standard. Heidegger sees this as the conduct's capacity to "hold up before itself" the binding force. Next this relationship is deepened in a temporal direction: Heidegger clarifies that, for this to occur, something must already have been done. The thing cannot provide a standard unless, in advance of our encountering it, we have already "leaped ahead" of ourselves, committed ourselves in advance to being bound by the standard afforded by the thing. This leap into a future has already taken place in the past. Earlier we read of an attunement by the thing and a self-opening to it. Now we ground all these relations in the leap ahead that was already accomplished, "holding up a binding force." The round shape of the coin will exercise a binding force for our conduct regarding it, and for our statement, but in advance the conduct must *permit* a binding force.

> **The ability of conduct to become attuned to that towards which it conducts itself comes about because this conduct can let itself be given a *standard* and a rule by anything towards which it is to conduct itself. How can this *standard-setting* come into play? Must it not be that the conduct has already, in advance, allowed that towards which it conducts itself to be standard-setting? The conduct must have already leaped ahead, in advance of itself; it must leap ahead to that towards which it is to conduct itself, and it must hold this up before itself as something binding. And it is this holding-up of a binding force that enables all conduct towards something to become self-engaged with standard-setting.** (p. 386)

Now Heidegger can speak of truth:

> **It is only because making statements is a mode of conduct that it can correspond, in its way, with that to which it is related, in its way. Being true as the revealing attunement to something [*Sichabstimmen auf*...] does not pertain to the statement *as* statement but to the statement *as* conduct.** (p. 385)

We have derived a self-opening of conduct and a revelatory power of conduct, so that rolling a coin or building a house can count as responsive and revelatory. The conduct has submitted to the thing; the conduct is **Such – As** the thing requires of it. The statement can *share in* these attributes of conduct because it is a form of conduct. There is no other possibility of responding or according than what conduct allows – Heidegger has said that conduct reveals our self-engagement with something, because only with conduct can the directive come into play. The statement is able to attune itself to a thing (*Sich-Abstimmen*) in a way that is revelatory, because as conduct it can correspond with its object (*übereinstimmen*). So being *true* is a possibility for every conduct, including statements. Why does this engagement of the conduct deserve to be called "being true, *Wahrsein*"? It is because such conduct fulfils the criteria established by the traditional word and concept of truth as we have assumed from the start, *adaequatio, übereinstimmen.* It is not a new concept of truth that we have here, but rather the discovery that truth is not primarily located in the statement. Conduct can be appropriate or inappropriate, with the capacity to assimilate a standard, and thereby be Such-As the thing requires. The inner standard within the conduct is the prototype of the truth of the statement. The traditional assignment of truth exclusively to statements as the sole essential locus of truth falls away. Truth does not originally reside in the proposition.

Here we have found yet another major Corner in our progress on the pathway. Up to this point we tied the very idea of truth to the statement. Now, with truth liberated from the statement and assigned to conduct, we must ponder further how we shall comprehend the essence of truth.

As the Section comes to its end, Heidegger considers the interaction of two elements within the conduct: the revealing of the thing, and on the other hand, the allowing of the binding force of the thing. The question is whether one of these is the condition of the other, that is, primordial. First of all, it seems that the revelatory power takes precedence, because if we did not have any access to the thing we could not discern in it anything that would exercise a binding. It could not be standard-setting. Yet there is reason to doubt this precedence – if a thing were neutrally revealed, without disclosure of any binding force in it, how could it then come to exercise a binding force? Must it not have inherently, in itself, the character of a binding force if the conduct is to come to respect it? He concludes the Section by arguing that no conduct would be able to become involved with a thing if there were not the binding power *and* the conduct's recognition of the binding power: the self-engaging becomes possible if one is *able* to acknowledge this binding force:

> **One point stands firm: one thing that makes it possible for conduct to become self-engaged with something is that it is always able to hold up before itself a binding force. The inner possibility of correspondence, i.e., truth, lies in holding up before one a binding force. Such an inner possibility of something [*possibilitas*] has long been recognized by philosophy, and with the best of reasons, as the essence of a thing [*essentia*].** (pp. 386–7)

The concluding sentence of our last quotation is portentous, and was by no means explained in context: This point will be taken up in Heidegger's next section and will concern us in the following two units of the exposition. Here a bit of historical information will supplement what Heidegger has told us now. He is invoking the idea of what makes truth possible. And this brings a major shift, or Corner, in the understanding of "essence." He will be asserting that "the essence of truth is freedom" in Section I(c), but already he has reinterpreted "essence":

> **The inner possibility of something [*possibilitas*] has long been recognized by philosophy, and with the best of reasons, as the essence of a thing [*essential*].**

This idea of that second stratum of the essence – possibility – is by no means Heidegger's invention – it reaches back all through the history of philosophy, though he does not say what chapters of that long history have inspired him. We can think of the rationalists of modern times. Alexander Baumgarten in his *Metaphysica*, Section 35,[50] says "the inner possibility of a thing is its essence." Other authors too had frequently spoken of the *essentia* of something as being equivalent to its *possibilitas*, often acknowledging (quite justifiably) inspiration from some of the Scholastic philosophers. See Leibniz, *Monadology*, nos. 42–5, which asserts that "there is a reality in essences or possibilities" (no. 44). For Leibniz, "God is the source not only of existences but also of essences, in so far as they are real, that is of all the reality there is in possibility" (no. 43). See also Christian Wolff, *Ontologia* no. 153: *per essentiam ens possible est.*[51]

How does the rationalist idea of essence find application to Heidegger's inquiry? Though the thing puts forward some aspect that serves as a standard, *Richtmass*, the thing's standard could never become authoritative for the statement by itself – that must be mediated by the conduct. The conduct that responds to the *Richtmass* and pre-gives the standard is also what guides the selection of aspects that, in our predicating statement, we choose to assign to the object: "The coin is *round*." The yielding to a binding force has been identified as the inner activity that yields the possibility of truth – thus, this "inner possibility" is the second stratum in the structure of this essence.

4. Freedom as Spontaneity: Section I(c) *(1930, pp. 387–90)*

Section I(c) opens with an inward turn that is also a backward turn. It is not self-evident that anyone can permit the binding power of a standard. Though the latter is a vital condition for the correspondence of the conduct, its own condition needs to be brought further to light. It is in a leaping ahead that one has taken on for oneself a binding through a standard; but to *permit* oneself to be bound, one must have *already* set oneself free for a binding. But is that self-explanatory? No. Who is in a position to set himself free? It is necessary to look further within.

The 1930 text is quite clear in distinguishing three different levels of the essence: there is the quiddity, and then, in Sec. I(b), its possibility (p. 387), and then, in Sec. I(c), the grounding for that possibility (p. 387), a third level identified by that Kantian term. Indeed, the Kantian influence will reach into the substance of this grounding too, for it is a freedom that recalls Kant's doctrine of spontaneity.

Hitherto we have seen that a standard can become binding upon us only if our conduct can "stand open" to a thing. But now we are going to see just how such an "open-standing conduct" can become possible in the first place. And the answer is: through freedom. Having explored this self-binding, we now probe into the *grounding* for *that* possibility – which will be the third stratum in the structure, or the architecture, of the essence. At this level, we can assert that "the essence of truth is freedom."

Heidegger has differentiated two terms: "inner possibility" and "ground of the inner possibility." The latter suggests a Kantian archetype. And indeed, just a year before, he had published *Kant and the Problem of Metaphysics* [*KM*],[52] which, especially in its introductory sections, made a very free use of the term *Wesen* in the same way we have just seen here: he is attempting a *Wesensbestimmung der Metaphysik* (pp. 19–20), which will establish the inner possibility, *innere Möglichkeit*, of such knowledge; moreover, the transcendental problem of the inner possibility of a priori synthetic knowledge is the question of the *Wesen der Wahrheit* of ontology (p. 26). In that book, Heidegger was confronting Kant with the "problem of metaphysics," and in doing so making his own combination of Kantian terms with those of an older metaphysics. He drew especially upon sources from the Leibniz–Wolff tradition in Germany (e.g., Baumgarten, whose book *Metaphysica* had served Kant himself as a textbook for his university lectures; *KM*, pp. 15–16). As we saw above, Baumgarten in his *Metaphysica*, Section 35, says "the inner possibility of a thing is its essence." Our 1930 text, then, seems to have appropriated the rationalists' account of essence, but also used Kant's famous term, "ground of the possibility." This might be seen as a hybrid variant of "essence," a rationalism modified by Kant.

> **To hold before oneself a binding force, one must have already set oneself free for a binding. But only because freedom is already at work can the conduct set itself free. It is this freedom that makes possible the inner leaping-ahead, through which all conduct is able to receive its standard. The ground of the inner possibility of the correspondence, i.e., of the common essence of truth, is freedom. Only with this third step in fathoming the ground of the inner possibility of the common essence have we got to the bottom of the essence of truth. The essence of truth is freedom.** (p. 387)

Our conduct can only adjust itself, accommodating the standard set by the thing, if it is free or open, ready to receive orientation. It is not forced into this mobile readiness by an external power, but it has freed itself, just through its attention to the object and its standard. Now at a further level, no conduct could accommodate itself to the object's standard unless it could set itself free, and the only possible route to freeing itself is by being already free. I cannot set myself free unless freedom is already at work in me, not the self-liberation that I am to achieve, but the freedom that is the antecedent condition for a self-liberation. And with this, he says, we have got to the bottom of the matter and further defined "essence." Here Heidegger has gone beyond Baumgarten and the other rationalists, to supplement them with a Kantian idea.

It is clear that our meditation has not been completed, for we hear immediately the note of doubt and criticism, this time objecting to this manner of rooting truth in freedom. We find in these lines another dialogue that begins by bringing up a trivial reading of the thesis that the essence of truth is freedom. Anyone could agree that speech acts must be like other kinds of acts: you have to be free to perform them, for you could also refrain from speaking if you chose. And agreeing or disagreeing with some utterance is just the same; we have to be free to do that whether or not that utterance is true. But Heidegger's thesis has nothing to do with communicative action or discursive behaviour, or with the kind of freedom they might manifest. We are not to reduce "the essence of truth" to "the essence of speech." To make freedom the essence of truth *itself* is a truly radical move, tying truth and falsity themselves down to human choices and wishes. Does it depend on our freedom that the coin actually *is* round or that the sea actually *is* salt? Such is the "forbidding" thesis that Heidegger expects us to fear.

So we are entertaining a further objection: truth is being reduced to a property of the human subject!

> **To place the essence of truth in freedom – does that not mean to abandon truth to human freedom? Can truth be more thoroughly undermined than by being sacrificed to human wish and will? Here something has come to the fore that was pressing on common sense during the whole discussion up to this point: truth is being reduced to a property of the human subject; man with his whims made into the measure of all things.** (p. 358)

This criticism is restated in several ways, but Heidegger seems to imagine that this objection is coming from the same antagonist – common sense – that he had confronted at the opening of the address. There at the beginning the antagonist was objecting to the abstractness and other-worldliness of philosophy and demanding a real, living, and practical truth. Is it credible that someone who has opposed philosophy in that spirit could now reverse himself to the extent of wanting to defend an absolute truth against the relativism apparently introduced by Heidegger? The two objections seem to pull in different directions. But it is actually quite common to find the two combined on different occasions where intellectuals have polemicized against philosophy. In our earlier objection from the partisan of "the real truth," we heard a doubt and denial of the possibility that philosophy has its own access to its own themes, such as the essence of anything – for example, of truth: we were supposed to stay close to the ground. In the present case, the antagonist is fearful of losing truth where it would become engulfed in subjectivity, and so is presumably defending the absoluteness of truth. But this time what the antagonist is defending is the independent, absolute truth of such assertions as "the coin is round," "the sea is salt." These are the *facts*, and this antagonist wants no part of a subjective or idealistic constitution of them; he always leads us back to the brass tacks.

This is an empiricism or atomism, and it is quite often heard where a critic denigrates the philosophical ascent to the "essence." We find this widely in our own culture. But we also hear it in past polemics against philosophy. F.H. Jacobi wrote polemics against Kant, Fichte, and Hegel in the years between 1795 and 1805, which seem to combine the two threads I have mentioned. On the one hand, he disputed the primacy they established for theoretical reason, insisting that it ignored the needs of daily life.[53] On the other, he claimed that we gain immediate access to sensible things, objects of our beliefs.[54] There are strong parallels in Jeremy Bentham, too, for whom metaphysics was just "nonsense on stilts," and who was also immune to any doubts about the empirical world. Perhaps this conjunction is characteristic of all empiricism – they attempt to interrupt the philosophical grasp of the absolute, yet they continue to insist on the real with its own kind of absolute. We find this on many occasions in history.

But we see that the antagonist is ready to say that every sort of *un*-truth can be attributed to human freedom, a misanthropic note that the critic introduces while denigrating philosophy (p. 389). Heidegger does not seem to dispute the point. He recalls the doctrine from the beginning that the theme of untruth can safely be left out of an investigation of the essence of truth. This is a timely reminder, for we shall soon find out that things are quite otherwise. In our Third Arc, we learn that untruth cannot be left aside, but belongs to the essence of truth.

Even philosophy itself, in its traditional form, can be invoked here to safeguard truth from contamination through human freedom – such philosophy as affirms eternal, unchanging truth. Just as Heidegger expressed respect for the doubts of his antagonist in the Introduction, so here he cannot "cast these doubts altogether aside." But, again in accord with the opening pages, he says the matter needs to be closely interrogated. Could it be that the antagonist has misunderstood the thesis, putting everything upside down (*verkehrt*)? But what reversal could Heidegger have in mind to put the matter straight?

Though we have been mentioning freedom throughout these pages, we have not yet asked what we mean by "freedom"; we have not inquired into *its* essence. In particular, we permitted ourselves to suppose that it is "a human property [*Eigenschaft*]," a commonsense doctrine, though it did not belong in any way to the argument. Anticipating the writings of Heidegger from the 1940s, we could call that a humanist doctrine of freedom. The objection we have been considering in recent pages proves to be based upon that assumption, and that is where the guiding thesis has become vulnerable.

> **The thesis is that the essence of truth is freedom. But as for freedom – is it a human property? That was no part of our claim. But we did not say, indeed we did not even ask, what freedom is. Hence the thesis remains questionable and exposed to the objections of common sense. So now our task is to rescue the claim that the essence of truth is freedom from the doubts posed by common sense.** (p. 389)

Just as we learned that truth is not located only in the statement, so we shall discover that freedom is not located in the human being. But of course the reader may wonder how freedom could be anything other than a human property – an issue to be taken up in Section II(a). Heidegger does not treat common sense as an external figure with which he can play, entangling it in the cords of dialectic – common sense has been recognized from the beginning as internal to philosophy. And so the rescue of the essence from common sense is internal to the meditation. The humanist assignment of freedom to the human subject continues to exercise its influence precisely within philosophy. But philosophy cannot rest with that assumption either.

This argument had been rehearsed in the short treatise, *On the Essence of Ground* [*WG*], 1929,[55] In the third section of the study, Heidegger argued that different forms of grounding – for example, causes and motives – are made possible by the projection of open possibilities, which is an act of freedom. With this open domain projected, we select from within it one ratio that is binding – to confront and to check a freedom is the very essence of a ratio or ground. Freedom constitutes the ratio as a limit to itself, so that Heidegger is able to say that the essence of ground is freedom.

Up to this point our thinking has described a curve. It began by affirming against all critics, and especially the down-to-earth realist, that we must investigate the essence of truth. We took an initial lead from the traditional philosophy that left traces in everyday language – truth is agreement or correspondence with a thing. But then, when we asked further how that was possible, we came to grasp that only practical conduct could assimilate a directive and thereby become capable of corresponding. And then we were led inside the constitution of this conduct to discover not only a self-liberation, but an antecedent freedom that made self-liberation possible. We have certainly left behind any dwelling in the abstractions of the clouds!

5. Freedom as Letting-Be: Section II(a)(i) *(1930, pp. 390–1)*

The concluding paragraph of Section I(c) prepares the way for a reversal, or Corner, that will be accomplished in Section II. Heidegger differentiates a preliminary apprehension of the essence from the adequate acknowledgment of it. The preliminary apprehension we have already accomplished is called a *Wesens-Bemächtigung.* This word signifies that we have got something in our grip, seized hold of it. That is what we accomplished with the three elements of essence we have already defined: (a) the word "accordance," which defines truth; (b) the inner possibility of the accordance, found in the allowing of a binding force; and (c) the a priori grounding in freedom.

But this was a mere preliminary to something else that is about to ensue in Section II, which he calls *Wesensermächtigung.* This word signifies empowering, as when a sovereign authorizes an ambassador to act, in general endowing a subject with the appropriate authority and scope. It applies here in that freedom is to be reconceived, freed from the prejudices of common sense, and put to work properly. This prepares an *Umkehr* to be accomplished in Section II, a reversal that overcomes the misunderstanding that has emerged. When that is done, we shall see how truth belongs to freedom. After thinking has made contact with the essence, what follows is to enable the essence (freedom) to become essential (*wesentlich*), to act in its full and complete essence (*in seinem vollen Wesen*). Only then is the essence "rescued." This reversal or *Umkehr* in the status of the essence marks the transition from the First to the Second Arc in the address. [Those are formal guidelines, and rather cumbersome in expression. This terminology will be dropped from the published text of 1949. It is by introducing a *further* essence, the essence of freedom, rather than by formally reversing the role of the essence in thinking, that the 1949 version will accomplish the switch from the First Arc to the Second Arc.]

The overturning of the commonsense and humanist assignment of freedom to the subject begins with this question: what view of the human being is implicit when freedom is taken to be a human property?

Now if we were to concede that truth and freedom were attributes of the human being, whence, on that assumption, would we derive the concept

> **of the human being? Is the human being nothing but this capricious and stubborn creature, equipped perhaps with reason, in whom truth is somehow, no doubt very poorly, lodged? Or what concept of humanity is one assuming?** (p. 390)

Common sense manifests a misanthropic stream that views it as improbable that this creature will ever know very much or accomplish much good. That is why people take offence at assigning freedom to be the condition for truth – one has to be suspicious of humanity and thus of freedom. But Heidegger once again acknowledges, with the same modesty, that his own inquiry is not free of equivalent difficulties. If he reproaches common sense for not investigating the grounds of its anthropology, his situation is no better, for he has not even once asked the obvious question: *If freedom is the essence of truth, what are we to understand by freedom?* Heidegger treats this as equivalent to the question of the essence of the human being. But now he is ready to say that the first part of the inquiry (the *Wesens-Bemächtigung*) has actually introduced us to the essence of freedom already, without calling explicit attention to it. We are already prepared for the reversal, the overturning:

> **The human being is not the bearer and possessor of freedom and truth, but everything is the other way around.** (p. 390)

Our earlier study showed the possibility of conduct (and therefore a statement) corresponding to a thing. We saw that the conduct had to assimilate a directive from the thing, or allow its binding force, which, because it entered into the conduct, could be called an inner directive. Heidegger raised a question earlier whether the revealing of the thing in question was required in advance for it to be able to exercise a binding force over us. He repeats here that this revealing does come first, but now he goes on to identify a further condition for this revealing. It is the *conduct* itself (*Verhalten*) that is to accomplish the revealing. We are not talking about a revealing accomplished by a disinterested, unsituated perception in advance of the conduct, nor of a prior revealing through scientific investigation. Why? Since the conduct is to be bound by the thing revealed, it must be present as the agent of the revealing. In what way, then, is conduct capable of revealing a thing? Conduct is deep-seated enough in our constitution that it is the grounding for all acts of perception and science, responsible for their revealing as well as for statements (as we have already seen). But it is not confined to those modes of revealing. When we engage in fashioning a statue or an implement, in repairing something, cleaning it, offering it for sale, and so on, our conduct is likewise engaged with the thing so as to reveal it. It is thus wrong to suppose that conduct becomes engaged with a thing *after* perception or science has revealed it antecedently. And each mode of conduct does experience the binding force emanating from the thing – the repair of an implement needs to be guided by what the thing ought to be. This is the revealing that lets the conduct correspond:

> **But what does that mean, that the conduct that relates itself to something must beforehand have revealed that being as a being? Nothing less than that the conduct must, in advance, have let that being be just the being that it is, and in the way that it is. A being could never have become revealed as a being, whether as an object or otherwise, if the conduct towards it had not already held to the stance of letting the being be.** (p. 391)

The conduct is receiving its directive and the binding force, so the corresponding stance of the conduct towards the thing is *letting it be.* So we have to understand the *allowing* of a binding force to be the very origin of letting-be. And the latter is keyed in to the very singular thing in question: it means letting the being be the being that it is and not another one. Can we then continue to hold that the revealing (accomplished by the conduct) takes place in advance of the allowing of a binding? The reasoning has shown that the relationship between these two factors is circular instead. The revealing permits the binding, but on the other hand we see that the revealing of a being through any mode of our conduct could not occur unless the conduct adhered to the stance of letting the being be, acknowledging the binding force. Soon we shall see that

> **the two aspects of all conduct that we have mentioned several times, revealing and the allowing of a binding, are after all not two but one and the same.** (p. 392)

The term *Seinlassen* has a negative sound in common speech, Heidegger points out, but that is quite opposed to his intention here. He claims that the original meaning of the term "letting-be" was broader and more positive. We can document this from many sources. Sometimes the term means "to allow something to be," for example, to be this or that; I can quote F.H. Jacobi again, who undertook to describe pure, empty space and said "I have to forget everything, including all movement, and I must *let* this forgetting … *be* the most important for me."[56] Sometimes the term means "to grant, in thinking, that a thing is such and such"; I can quote a passage where Luther interprets the Genesis creation account in terms of his *Logos* Christology: we have to *let* the word *be* different from God the speaker (*Er muss das Wort etwas anderes sein lassen denn Gott, seinen Sprecher*), but we also have to *let* this Word *be* God (*So muss er's gewisslich auch Gott sein lassen*).[57] But Heidegger has a more positive and potent idea of letting-be than any previous thinker. That is the force of his attention to *being*.

Letting-be is oriented to the singular thing – as we said above, the term means letting the being be the being that it is and not some other one. But along with that, when a conduct engages in letting a being be, it understands the being *of* that being. But it does not derive that understanding of being empirically from its encounter with that singular thing. Being is not a predicate in the way that "round" and "salt" are. What is especially salient to letting-be is that it warrants the encounter as the revealing of the thing; the encounter only counts as a revealing because it opens up the being of the thing. And it is because the encounter is a letting-be that we can speak significantly of this coin *as a being*. While it certainly is a thing and an object as well, it holds its status as a being because the revealing is a letting-be. The letting-be takes place because there was, in advance of the encounter, the allowing of a binding force, an open-ended, general preparedness for each specific binding force that it will experience. Therein lies the advance anticipation of the being of whichever being will appear. This shows that to all human conduct there belongs an antecedent understanding of being, which inveighs against the obliviousness to being that is also a constant human possibility. It is because of the antecedent understanding of being that human beings are able to nurture and to save the beings they encounter. Heidegger will call that the human self-engagement with beings.

[But while in 1930 Heidegger sees the grounding for our recognition of the *being* of the beings that we can let be to lie in the human antecedent understanding of being – serving as an a priori for our encounter with them – we shall be seeing in Part II, Unit 4, that in 1943 and 1949 Heidegger is no longer content with that account of the matter. The reasons for this change will begin to appear at the end of Part I below.]

Here we have turned explicitly to the theme of being – we shall look further into the theme of being guided by the perspective of "letting-be." It is noteworthy that this idea of freedom has taken on a leading role in 1930 in guiding the account of being. Von Herrmann has called attention to this, finding here a major shift from the viewpoint of *SZ*: where *SZ* was committed to viewing time (or temporality) as the determining meaning of being, *Sinn von Sein*, there is a change in 1930, both in the lectures[58] and in the present address, where it is freedom – in the form of letting-be – that serves as the *Sinn von Sein*. As for freedom, we are granting it its full force, its empowerment as the essence of truth, which will become explicit at the end of II(a). Here the open scope that permits conduct is the essence of freedom, and it expresses itself in the relationship we can take up to things. Freedom is a relationship, letting-be, not an interior property of the human being. Thus the original letting-be opens up the being of the things – and it is decisive for our own being as well. It governs how we understand our being. But we cannot occupy that zone without encountering all the other things that occupy it as well – there is no unmixed experience of the open zone, but only letting something be.

The Second Arc of the address, starting from freedom, lasts all through Section II(a), where we discover what are the grounds of the possibility of freedom, and what broader, even cosmic, dimensions are implied by it. This change of direction will culminate in an entirely new version of the essence of truth, a discovery prompted by our insights into essence, our grasping of it, and our putting it to work – the interaction between thinking and essence.

6. Truth as Unconcealedness – The Greek Beginning: Section II(a)(ii) *(1930, pp. 391–2)*

This unit introduces the Unconcealed, and it does so following in the train of the preceding exposition: we have spoken of the conduct that undergirds our intending and our utterance; we have sought to derive the truth of the conduct and utterance through the leaping ahead, that which permits a binding through the object, or rather, through the being; this was the "allowing of a binding" whereby we have permitted the norm or standard to radiate from the being and bind us. Such an intention is called "letting-be." We read of the general, antecedent openness that precedes each encounter: the "original letting-be of beings"; our conduct becomes possible because of the clearing, the scope, opened up by it. And now a revealing of the things becomes possible through it, what Heidegger calls first unconcealedness (*Unverborgenheit*) and then deconcealment (*Entborgenheit,* his neologism). The conduct itself would not be possible without this:

> **This original letting-be of beings as such brings about, in advance, the open clearing for all conduct and the site where it can gain a foothold. It is in the letting-be of beings as such that such a thing as a being ever becomes unconcealed, that is, de-concealed. The unconcealed was known to Western philosophy in its decisive beginning with Heraclitus as *ta alēthea.* We are accustomed to translate the Greek *alētheia* [unconcealedness, or better, de-concealedness of beings] as "truth." Now we see, on the basis**

> **of the inner development of the essence of correspondence, that what we unthinkingly call truth is the de-concealedness of a being as such, and that this occurs through the letting-be of beings. This letting-be of beings is in itself de-concealing-revealing. And because letting beings be as beings is their unveiling, revealing, this also lets them be binding, namely, as beings in their being. And again only because beings in their being are binding do they show themselves as beings. The two aspects of all conduct that we have mentioned several times, revealing and the allowing of a binding, are after all not two but one and the same.** (pp. 391–2)

It is only in this Second Arc that Heidegger introduces Greek terminology: the collective term *ta alēthea,* the things that lie unconcealed; and the abstract noun *alētheia,* unconcealedness itself (or deconcealedness) of beings. The philosophical argument up to this point has derived the idea of unconcealedness. Only after that is *granted* do we make our excursion back to the archaic period of Greece where we find these prototypical words. The argument we have reviewed up to this point does not depend on any philology or etymology. Throughout the early pathway of his thinking, Heidegger displays confidence that his phenomenology is able to interpret the thought of the ancients, whether Aristotle or the Presocratics. So the Greek word finds its exegesis here through this action: our letting-be is able to de-conceal beings because it allows their binding force – that is, *alētheia.* This interpretation has two aspects: modern philosophy is given a hermeneutical advantage over ancient philosophy; and free human conduct is made into a condition for the unconcealedness of beings. [In the 1949 version, we shall see that this relationship is reversed: unconcealedness becomes the condition for our letting-be – See Part II, Unit 6.]

Next we shall explore this *alētheia,* but before doing so we may try to clarify its relation to the initial quiddity of truth: accordance. We are being told now that the historical and primordial essence of truth was unconcealedness. But it seems that our freedom gives us access to beings in their unconcealedness whenever we are capable of letting them be. Only that which is unconcealed can exercise the binding function whereby our intending and our speaking can achieve accordance. Thus, and to that extent, our conduct recapitulates the experience of the ancient Greeks. The essence of truth incorporates this history.

As for the philology, the scholarly literature surrounding Heidegger may have left some readers in doubt whether *alētheia* really should be translated *Unverborgenheit* = unconcealedness. We should be able to remove this doubt. I commented on many of Heidegger's texts, and on some of the ensuing philological debates about *alētheia,* in the essay "On the Manifold Meaning of Truth in Aristotle," and showed that those who had criticized Heidegger on this score had been effectively answered by classicists who came to his defence.[59] There is, of course, the further doubt to be treated – whether this Greek term really is an expression for truth; and obviously, that entails the further philosophical question whether truth itself can be understood as unconcealedness.

Heidegger does not dispute the rendering of *alētheia* as "truth": philosophy is an inquiry into its essence. It is showing how freedom is empowered to induce the self-unveiling of beings; once we understand that, we shall then be prepared to study whether that phenomenon really is truth. The Greek word is offering some guidance in this study.

How do his texts understand this Greek word? (a) He treats it as a composite word, a negative word, an alpha-privative added to a root *-lēthē*; (b) it appears as adjective (*alēthes*), noun (*alētheia*), and verb (*alētheuein* – especially in Aristotle); (c) the roots *-lēthē*, *-lath-*, and *lanthanomai* signify "be hidden," "concealment," and "forgetting"; (d) the composite word signified "unconcealment," rendered by a number of different German words, and therefore English ones as well, varying from "revealedness" to "unveiling" to "disclosing"; (e) this affords the concept of truth in the Greek language and Greek philosophy; and (f) when *alēthēs* is attributed to the soul, to one of the intellectual virtues, or to a statement, it means "true," but when attributed to the object it means "unconcealed." It arises through the tearing off of a veil, always preceded by a concealment enshrouding the subject. Most centrally, unconcealment always preserves some relationship to concealment; it does not abolish it utterly; there is some sort of continuity between them, and, in consequence, some continuity between truth and untruth. This implication of the positive role of concealment and untruth will be our theme as we treat the Third Arc. In Heidegger this is no antiquarian point – Greek philosophy with its concept of truth is to be exemplary for us and our philosophy. *WW* is inquiring into the essence and constitution of this.

We have to ask whether he is right on points (a) to (f). His work has not stood unchallenged. On (a), Friedländer, in the second edition of his book on Plato,[60] said that there was no clear evidence that this was an alpha-privative word; it is likely that "*alēthēs* has nothing to do with *-lēthē*, *-lath-*, *lanth*" (p. 222). Thus we could hardly find "a passage in which the object of the verb could be (let alone must be) the 'unhidden'" (p. 223). Thus Friedländer disposes of points (d), (e), and (f) as well. But his analysis was refuted by a paper by Heitsch, a Göttingen classicist, that appeared in 1962.[61] In a matter such as this, as he explains, the objective history of word-formation – what is usually called etymology – is not as important as the understanding the ancient authors (whose texts we possess) had of the relationships among the words they used, how, for example *they* treated the relationship of *alētheia* to *lēthē*, *-lath-*, *lanth*, and so on. And from non-philosophers from Homer on down through the tragedians, historians, and rhetoricians, he assembles about twenty passages showing that *alētheia* is an alpha-privative word: the word-relations in the texts show that the authors placed it in strong contrast to *lēthē* and its cognates. He then adds about a dozen quotations from Plato showing the same thing – for example, from *Apology* 17 a, "they almost made me forget who I was [*epelathomēn*] ... and yet they hardly uttered a word of truth [*alēthes*]." The grammarians of later antiquity who codified this relationship were only reflecting the word use that had prevailed for centuries (Heitsch, p. 26); moreover, this interpretation of *alētheia* has been standard in classical scholarship since Johannes Classen in the 1850s (p. 24). Other papers, too, have appeared[62] that establish that *alētheia* does mean truth and that it is a privative construction. When Friedländer came to issue a third edition of his book,[63] he acknowledged (pp. 234–7, 386–7) that Heitsch had established his case; the reproaches against Heidegger were unjustified.

The 1930 address attributes the two forms of the Greek word to Heraclitus, though in fact we do not find either form of the word among his extant fragments.[64] [The name of Heraclitus is dropped from the equivalent passage of the 1943 and 1949 publications, **4.3.** But in **4.5.**, Heidegger does speak of "the first thinker taking a questioning stand with regard to the unconcealment of beings," and the context suggests it is Heraclitus he means.] Heidegger is probably justified in linking *alētheia* to Heraclitus, because we find the related, contrasting word *lathoi* in the Diels Fragment 16: "How could anyone hide [*lathoi*] from that which never sets?"[65] And he would probably have referred to it in some lines of the poem that have been lost; moreover, some attributions from later antiquity[66] testify to his interest in and views about *alētheia*. *Alētheia*, such a famous word, is most prominently inscribed in Parmenides.

When it becomes possible for us to reveal beings *as beings*, they have become unconcealed for us (*unverborgen* – which Heidegger also calls *entborgen*). Where a thing or object is not apprehended as a being, it is still concealed. Letting-be is what reveals. We can express Heidegger's present point by showing how phenomenology would reverse the doctrines of Kant. The "phenomenon" is the being that shows itself along with its very being (we recall that the latter is the "phenomenon of phenomenology"). It is brought into the open by our freedom, our letting-be. But the "thing in itself," what has not become unconcealed through our letting-be, is the mass of real or material determinations contained in a thing. The thing in itself retreats into itself as the non-phenomenon.

We may note that when our conduct is understood to engage in unconcealment, the difference between revealing- and allowing-a-binding disappears; that problem is solved.

Heidegger's account comes to its provisional conclusion: we are to understand truth as unconcealedness, *alētheia.*

> **Freedom, understood as the letting-be of beings as such has now come to the fore to help constitute the essence of truth in the sense of the deconcealedness of beings. Truth is no mere subjective occurrence in a proposition, but the revealed exposure to the revealed beings as such. All human conduct is revelatory in this way or that, and engages itself with that towards which it conducts itself. Thus it must have received its endowment – the inner directive – from the restraint that informs all letting-be, that is, from freedom. The human being exists: now that means that he is in the truth, standing exposed in the revealedness of beings as such.** (p. 384)

The present treatment remains consistent with the approach Heidegger took to the ancient and modern terms in *SZ.* Heidegger mentions this Greek word in *SZ,* on page 219, and I retranslate for emphasis:

> **The translation [of the word *alētheia*] by means of the word "truth," and even more our theoretical-conceptual determinations of this expression ["truth"], cover up the meaning of what the Greeks accepted as "self-evident": the pre-philosophical understanding of *alētheia* that lay at the basis of their terminological employments of the term.**

So while the Greeks understood *alētheia* pre-philosophically as unconcealedness, and while their philosophers' writings (he has been referring to Aristotle and Heraclitus) preserved and reflected this understanding through their terminology, modern translations and terminology (*Wahrheit*), and especially modern concepts and theories, have covered these matters up. But in fact Heidegger was introducing this Greek terminology on page 219 in order to give his *own* theory an ancient pedigree. *SZ* shows that there are phenomenological grounds for understanding truth as disclosure or uncovering or revealing – the statement is true through uncovering beings.[67] This phenomenology can be appraised as it stands independently of Greek scholarship; it is not generated entirely out of his exegesis of the Greek words, but supposedly confirmed by them. Thus, to some degree, *Dasein*'s uncovering was anticipated in the ancient *alētheia.* Later he will back away from this identification,[68] arguing that modern phenomenological concepts are an imperfect means for grasping ancient Greek experience, but in the present context we can acknowledge that the 1930 address resembles *SZ* in being ready to assimilate Greek terminology to the assumptions of the phenomenological method.

There is, of course, doubt and debate, not only about the etymology of the Greek word, but also about whether this Greek term really is an expression for truth. Obviously, whether truth itself can be understood as unconcealedness is a philosophical question. Heidegger said that it was an "unthinking" translation merely to render this term as "truth": what he has in mind is the habit of using lexicons to make automatic translations from the texts of authors from earliest times on, through Plato and Aristotle, up through late antiquity. He is rightly impatient with conventional interpretations (and there are many other cases of similarly thoughtless, conventional translation: *logos* = word; *ousia* = substance; *psychē* = soul; etc.). But it is no remedy to substitute other, novel translations, and Heidegger does not dispute the rendering of *alētheia* as "truth." But as he says in 1949, it is not merely more literal to translate "unconcealedness" – it brings before us the "still uncomprehended factor of de-concealedness."

We see from another tradition the critique by Bernard Williams.[69] His view is that it is a confusion in philosophy to suppose there could be diverse concepts of truth – everyone always means the same thing by "true," and this has been adequately explained, and "proved," by Tarski: *p* is true if and only if *p*. In his Afterword, he turns to the ancient Greeks. *Alētheia* was their most common word, though there were others (*eteos, etymos*, etc.), and though by its etymology it might be thought to mean "unconcealedness," it would be illusory to think it actually meant that. Since it undoubtedly does mean "true," it cannot mean anything else, for we know that in all languages and all times, people mean the same thing by "true" – that things are indeed so. Williams does not argue for this reading of *alētheia*: it just means "true," and there's an end of it. Heideggerianism is just a "sectarian" philosophy (p. 273).

The philosophical presupposition of Williams (as distinct from the philological) is that if *alētheia* means *X*, then it cannot also mean *Y* and *Z*. He insists on a univocal meaning: "Everything is what it is, and not another thing" (Bishop Butler). But Heidegger's essence, *Wesen*, has a complex constitution, incorporating not only the quiddity and the ground of its possibility but also the history in which the original formation of truth was transmitted, albeit in a concealed form. This is history as fate, which reaches out from antiquity to comprehend us with our "usual concept of truth." Part II of this book will deal with the history of the complex constitution of truth, beginning from *alētheia*.

7. *Da-sein* the Human Essence: Section II(a) (iii) *(1930, pp. 392–4)*

The remainder of II(a) treats together the four themes *Dasein*, Existence, Nature, and History. Heidegger assigns many achievements to his "letting-be of beings." This "letting-be of beings" is described as a venture, or a wager, in which the human being rises up in the midst of the world with a challenge to it – that it reveal itself:

> **The letting-be of beings is not that sort of indolence that would just let them slip away; rather, it lets it seriously count that beings as such are, and that nothingness is not. This letting-be is a daring venture that places its all – not just this or that – on the venture of rising up in the midst of beings, and standing forth against them all. The uprising against them is not to conquer them or to diminish them – the uprising is not a rebellion; but rather this rousing oneself against beings as such holds itself in check so as, in this restraint, to let the beings be – what? What they are, and in the way that they are.** (p. 392)

The challenge is that the world should reveal itself *as being*, which is to say not as non-being. It is the venturing challenger who carries the expectation that beings should *be*, and must *be*; it seems thus to be the challenger who is furnished in advance with the understanding of being, measuring the beings by it. This Promethean uprising is not, however, a rebellion or an attack on beings: it is marked by a self-restraint, holding itself in check. What could Heidegger have in mind with this combination of uprising and restraint? His words here recall the account of science that he offered in his 1929 inaugural lecture, "What Is Metaphysics?"[70] Science was (a) an irruption, *Einbruch*, into the totality of beings, that forces them to disclose themselves to the investigator. But it was also (b) that attentive posture that gave to the things themselves the first and last word, where "a submission to beings themselves obtains, such that beings are allowed to reveal themselves" – what he could have called there, but did not, "letting them be." So the present lecture takes one further step beyond 1929 by characterizing this scientific practice as the structure of *truth*. Heidegger is also prepared to say here that our challenge to the world helps the beings become what they are, "liberating them to be what they are," the idea of *SZ*, Section 43(c), that while beings do not depend upon *Dasein*, it is through *Dasein* that the being *of* beings is constituted. Here that means that the things could not set standards (*Massgabe*) and express their power without us, which we know is interior to truth.

In *SZ*, within the discipline of fundamental ontology, the term *Mensch* had been avoided, replaced by the ontological term *Dasein*. A characteristic declaration was:

> **This being which we ourselves in each case are and which includes inquiry among the possibilities of its being we formulate terminologically as Dasein.** (*SZ*, p. 7)

Heidegger did not long continue in the usage of *SZ*. He had already moved away from the earlier strict fundamental-ontological mode of expression in some lectures before 1930: for instance, he spoke of "the *Dasein* in man today" in his course of 1929.[71] The 1930 address uses the term *Mensch* frequently, and it is only in Section II(a) that he introduces the term *Dasein*. In 1930 this term is not *substituted* for *Mensch* as it had been in *SZ*; rather we see that, by virtue of human freedom as letting-be, the human being can attain through *Dasein* a new possibility of existence:

> **It is in our freedom – the letting-be of beings as such – that the human being accomplishes existence itself. With this accomplishment, the human being is now really standing exposed over against other beings ... This is a real counter-posing of one being to another one, to a being that has become revealed, and we call this counter-posing the *Dasein* of the human being. Through freedom, as the letting-be of beings as such, the human being becomes liberated for an existence as *Da-sein*.** (p. 393)

The term "Da-sein" is central to all of Heidegger's work, early and late, but whereas in *SZ Da-sein* was (usually) the human being, in *WW*, when thinking explores the *essence* of truth, it will establish *Da-sein* as the *essence* of the human being. [See also below, Part II, Unit 6.] In *SZ*, the word *Da-sein* was *mainly* used (90 per cent of the time) in a concrete or ontic sense, to designate the being that exists (ourselves). I've introduced the noun "exister" to take the place of this use of the word *Da-sein*.[72] Since we alone, among all beings, *exist*, one can apply the term "exister" to the human being. To the despair of translators, *Da-sein* in *SZ* also has at times an impersonal, ontological sense, signifying the *mode of being* that characterizes ourselves. Many phrases in *SZ* – for example, in Sections 26, 27, 29, and 31 – have that sense. In this second application, it coincides with the ontological term *Existenz*, both in traditional discourse and in Heidegger's text. Even though its original etymology (Being-there or Being-here) may suggest other connotations to a German reader, that does not affect the phenomenology of *SZ*. In the remaining pages here, then, when I refer to the *exister*, I shall sometimes add the word *Da-sein* in brackets, where it will have the ontic sense, and at times I'll follow the same practice with the word "existence," the ontological sense. (In 1930 there may be some uncertainty over this: at points it does seem to treat *Dasein* as subject of verbs of action, as if it were equivalent to *der Mensch*). We see that in the last paragraph quoted above Heidegger first spelled the term without a hyphen, but in a later line inserted a hyphen, and this indicates a transition to viewing *Da-sein* as *Ek-sistenz*, not designating the human being but characterizing the *essence* of the human being.

If letting-be is a self-restraining uprising, we now learn that this is the very character of human existence, or *Ex-sistenz* (the Latin spelling he uses in 1930 for what he later called *Ek-sistenz*). Existence is a moving-out-of-self, a moving out in front of things. The discussion has been focused on the letting-be of some singular being, such as a coin, though there was certainly a general openness on our part in approaching that being. *But now it is beings as a whole to which we are open.* The perspective opens upon a *world*, to which the ancients gave the name of *physis*. Our letting-be moves out in front of things and the world as a whole, exposing itself to them.

Our own exposure to the things and the world is not only our existence, it is our freedom, which could not be a mere interior condition. Freedom is not our attribute; it is now identified both with existence and with the open sphere in which the things and world display themselves. That gives Heidegger occasion to deny the "commonsense" idea of freedom, as an ability to incline this way or that.

Being exposed to things gives Heidegger a way of explaining his term *Da-sein* with an emphasis on the "There," the *Da*, our location; now we know where *Da-sein* is – in front of things, and in front of the whole world, exposed. The discussion concludes with a turn again to antiquity. It was a Greek philosopher who did more than discover and inaugurate existence. *The same act was the revelation of nature (physis) and also the initiation of history.* History, nature, and existence were all comprehended in the epochal opening up of the being of beings – beings *as a whole* – Heidegger's appraisal of the world-historical triumphs of the archaic period in Greek history. This existence of the human being began at that moment when the first thinker rose up with the question, What are beings in themselves? Heidegger speaks of "the first thinker taking a questioning stand with regard to the unconcealment of beings," and the context suggests it is Heraclitus of whom he speaks. With this question, what beings as such are, unconcealedness was for the first time experienced as such, though not comprehended: the ancients comprehended beings, but not the unconcealedness that governed their thinking. With all these limitations, it remains nevertheless true that this was the essential discovery in all human history, and inaugurated the era in which we too still stand. We comprehend unconcealedness though our study of letting-be and freedom, and the remainder of this essay will go much further into it. Human liberation for existence as *Da-sein* began with this question about beings, and in this liberation nature, in the original sense of *physis*, first unveils itself, and with this liberation history first begins. History, nature, and existence were all comprehended in the epochal opening up of the being of beings. Heidegger always stresses that *physis* was a word for being itself, or for the whole world, not just one sector of it, for example, what we call "nature" as differentiated from history or society or consciousness. By analogy to what we have already said about one's dealings with ordinary things, we may understand the thinker's question, too, as a venture or irruption into the open and as a self-exposure to beings as a whole. Therefore, we may regard his question too as a letting-be: the letting-be of beings as a whole. This question was just as much an act of freedom as is any conduct towards a particular thing. Indeed, Heidegger speaks of it here as if it were an utterly original and unmotivated act.

Early Greek thinking focused on *physis* or being, and did so within the frame of the openness of beings in totality, that is, seeing them encompassed within *alētheia*, even though they did not turn the focus of their attention upon *alētheia* itself. Why is that earlier study relevant here? Once the primordial totality of being has been revealed, that revelation has *not been cancelled out or utterly abrogated or rescinded.* There remains the "openness of beings as a whole" *even if we today cannot apprehend it, even if, for us, it has receded behind the summative totality of modern science.*

8. Truth and Concealedness – Attunement: Section II(b)(i) *(1930, pp. 395–6)*

Where the first arc led us from the traditional definition of truth (adequation) to what makes adequation possible (free conduct assimilating a directive); and where the second arc proceeded from this freedom to the unconcealedness of beings that we can let be, now a further movement begins that bends our thinking away from the unconcealed beings. This cuts the address in half, for all the remainder will continue to move inexorably away from the unconcealment of beings. Two movements of thought are completed before we come to the end, both of which manifest the role of untruth within the essence of truth. Heidegger says that the essence of untruth must belong to the essence of truth. This is in defiance of common sense, which would hold, as we saw at the very beginning, that untruth can be of no interest to a study of truth. Untruth takes on various forms. First, the *concealment* of things: the unconcealment of beings depends on and includes a concealment of them. This is the non-truth that Heidegger calls the Non-essence (*Unwesen*) of truth, or the "essence of untruth," *Wesen der Unwahrheit.* Then, we shall encounter a second form of untruth, erring (*die Irre*), also incorporated in the essence of truth. *Die Irre* proves to have a multitude of varieties [but they can all be grouped together, in a formulation first introduced in 1943 and 1949, as the "essential counter-essence" (*das wesentliche Gegenwesen*) of truth].

> **But because truth is essentially freedom, the human being engaged in letting the beings be can also not let them be the beings that they are, in the way that they are. The beings become covered up, distorted – more exactly, they become concealed, in one way or another, un-true.** (p. 394)

Freedom as the essence of truth was not suspended by the movement of the Second Arc: it was still freedom that let the unconcealed beings be. But out of this conjunction arises a new reversal. We also have the free option not to let them be, to "cover over and distort them." We have discovered a double potential of freedom, and so truth must inherit such doubleness:

> **But if the essence of truth as freedom becomes essential in that way for our existence as such, what of the status of untruth: can it just be left out as unessential? Or must not this Non-essence of truth belong precisely to the essence of truth? Then, if the essence is to realize its full scope and authority over us, would it not have to retrieve this Non-essence, i.e., untruth, and admit it explicitly into the essence of truth? Certainly! Admitting the Non-essence into the essence is not a secondary adjunct to the insight into the essence, something that could in principle be left out. Rather, admitting the Non-essence into the essence is an integral part of granting the authority of the essence, as the second step.** (p. 394)

At this abstract level, we should note that there is a current in Heidegger scholarship[73] that warns against a close companionship between truth and untruth, fearing that this would erode the norms of discourse and endanger justice and liberty. But that is to overlook the status of essence in Heidegger's thought: if untruth is included in the essence, that does not mean that something untrue would now be recognized as true. In the following study we shall see what does follow from including untruth within the essence of truth. His remarks on untruth give us a further insight into essence: while a cat is not a dog, the *essence* of cat does not exclude the dog or the dog's essence in the same way. This was also true of Plato's ideas: they had an interweaving (*symplokē*) in such a way that, for example, the idea of Motion had a positive relation to the idea of Rest (*Sophist* 251–2). Likewise, Heidegger's essence of truth – we shall be seeing in detail – incorporates several variants of untruth.

Because of freedom there is an equal role for untruth within the essence of truth. That must provoke a reflection here: does the responsible initiative for the two possibilities lie entirely with us, with the human being? Would that not imply the subjectivist, humanist doctrine of freedom that was abandoned in the Second Arc? Descartes, in his Fourth Meditation, could derive falsity from the freedom of the human subject, its will surpassing its store of clear and distinct ideas. But, in Section II(a), we have already seen the human subject not as the root of freedom but as overshadowed by freedom – that was the very beginning of the Second Arc. If it is due to freedom that untruth is admitted into the essence, it cannot be because of the human being's exercise of free choice.

Now if the topic is the essence of untruth, we require preparation for that move: we need to understand what there is in the essence of *truth* that leads into untruth – why is there a stratum that belongs to the essence of truth that *is not* truth? We summon up our strength first of all for a leap into untruth in the first of the two senses: concealment,[74] moving beyond the generic concept of untruth to this specific form, *die Verborgenheit*. Let us take note of the *Corners* of the pathway: now thinking begins to bend away from *alētheia*, an irruption of untruth into the essence of truth. The pathway begins to move from the Unconcealed to the Concealed. The central question the reader must confront is: Why? What is the reason for this coming eclipse of *alētheia*?

As we proceed we must keep in mind the key provisions that have already been touched on, summarized near the end of II(a):

> **Freedom, understood as the letting-be of beings as such has now come to the fore to help constitute the essence of truth in the sense of the de-concealedness of beings. Truth is no mere subjective occurrence in a proposition, but the revealing exposure to the revealed beings as such. All conduct is revelatory in this way or that.** (p. 394)

In treating true statements, Heidegger does not see the speaker as detached from his milieu, and he does not speak of beliefs as if they were the truth-bearers. The key word in all his works on this theme is *das Da-sein*, and we are to imagine *Da-sein*, the exister, as thrust forward into his milieu in close encounters: truth is an attribute of the existence of the exister.

A crucial aspect of the analysis is that we enter into a relationship with a thing through our conduct, *Verhalten* – this term has also been translated as "comportment." Heidegger's account thus allows a place for action in the account of truth, which recalls the treatment of circumspective concern and being-in-the-world in *SZ*: through our conduct, we are able to be open to the thing and respond to the criterion it sets, a prototype of the statement's truth. In treating the conjunction of the revealing with the revealed, the very exposure of the human being to the beings, he develops a duality on the side of the beings: on the one hand, there is "this being or that one," and on the other, there is the totality of beings, *das Seiende im Ganzen*.

The conduct of the human being, even as it engages this being or that, is in every case marked or attuned, *gestimmt*, precisely by the totality of beings, *das Seiende im Ganzen*.

> **In every conduct something further is always contained. Every conduct of the human being is attuned, whether emphatically or not, and through this attunement it is absorbed into the totality of beings. A given conduct of a human being need not have taken special cognizance of this totality of beings that surrounds all conduct.** (p. 395)

The particular problem addressed here is that there is a role for untruth in the essence of truth, one kind of untruth in particular – concealment, *Verbergung*. Once we have seen that the exister's conduct is attuned, we shall grasp that attunement incorporates concealment. On this matter I can contrast Heidegger with other possible views – for example, that of Critical Philosophy, which asserts that our knowledge is inherently limited because of our own finite faculties. But Heidegger's case is different.

The first step is to explore the role of the conduct of the human being. The conduct of the human being is in every case marked or attuned, *gestimmt*, precisely by the totality of beings, *das Seiende im Ganzen*:

> **Every human conduct pulses within the letting-be of beings so that it can engage in conduct towards this being or that one. And yet! In every conduct something further is always contained. Every conduct of the human being is attuned, whether emphatically or not, and through this attunement it is absorbed into the totality of beings. A given conduct of a human being need not have taken special cognizance of this totality of beings that surrounds all conduct. This revealedness of beings in their totality does not coincide with the sum of beings that are actually known. On the contrary, where beings are only slightly known, and only very roughly discerned by science, the revealedness of beings in their totality can be more powerful than where**

> **what is known and at any time knowable has grown beyond all bounds; where nothing can withstand the drive to know; where there is no limit to the purely technical mastery of things. Precisely in a flat, prosaic know-it-all and nothing-but-knowing there is lacking the revealedness of beings in their totality.** (p. 395)

We must retain this point: two different ideas of totality, *das Ganze*, are treated in this paragraph. On the one hand, we read that where very little of the world has been explored by science, the openness or manifestness of the totality of beings can prevail effectively. Let us call this a primordial wholeness. But on the other hand, there is the sum total of objects that "are actually known" (*Summe des gerade bekannten Seienden*). This is highly relevant in a scientific modernity, a summative sense of *das Ganze*, because in modernity nothing can any longer escape the drive to knowledge and technological mastery. In modern life, the primordial totality has receded; it has become ungraspable and indeterminate, a primordial wholeness that has vanished behind the summative totality (even though the latter is also never realized). We can compare this to Heidegger's earlier work, for the primordial wholeness coincides with what he called the "world" in *SZ* and *WG*. Heidegger avoids this term in *WW*, but we shall use it at times to refer to the primordial wholeness. What is operative in the primordial wholeness or world is its revealedness, *Offenbarkeit*, or openness, *Offenheit*, both terms used in 1930. Thinking no doubt of simpler times in antiquity, he reinforces the point by saying that this kind of revealedness is at work even more powerfully where the stock of cognitions is fairly modest:

> **[W]here beings are only slightly known, and only very roughly discerned by science, the revealedness of beings in their totality can be more powerful than where what is known and at any time knowable has grown beyond all bounds.**

Heidegger has already treated this primordial wholeness in Section II(a), where he recounted the discoveries of the early Greek philosophers. We should recall that, in *SZ*, there is an existential distinction between understanding, *Verstehen*, and interpretation, *Auslegung*. A primary thesis of *SZ* was that all *Auslegung* is made possible by a primary *Verstehen*. In this way too we can characterize the distinct ways in which *Da-sein* here in *WW* grasps these two versions of totality. The world or the primordial totality is projected through *Da-sein*'s understanding or *Verstehen*, while all the distinct things we seize upon in experience and science are grasped by way of interpretation, *Auslegung*.

Heidegger has said in the longer quotation above that all human conduct – including, of course, the making of statements – is attuned (*gestimmt*) precisely by the totality of beings, that is, by the primordial totality, or world. This is in its origin a kind of unconcealment of things, in accord with the original disclosure of antique thought, but a deeper consideration of the matter will make it apparent that such attunement is actually a concealment.

Besides the objective duality that we stressed in the foregoing paragraphs – this or that being versus the totality of beings – Heidegger introduces a duality within the human being, in *Da-sein*. The human being engages in conduct, *Verhalten*, that we see is essential to truth. Yet the human being is also marked by freedom, and this becomes interpreted here as "letting-be," *Seinlassen*. We can say that the whole argument works by tracing the correlation between the two dualities: (1) the duality between a given being and the whole, the world; and (2) the duality in *Da-sein* between letting-be and conduct.

Heidegger clarifies in Section II(a) that letting-be is the broader condition for conduct, and in II(b) he repeats the point:

> **Every human conduct pulses, *schwingt*, within the letting-be of beings, so that it can engage in conduct towards *this being or that one*.** (p. 395)

We turn attention now to the second element within the human power of revealing, the letting-be:

> **If the letting-be of beings sustains the conduct, it penetrates it thoroughly and outreaches it, and, in outreaching, it reaches up to beings in their totality.** (p. 395)

Letting-be, in all its originality, is guiding the conduct, but it contains within it a more primordial relationship – to the totality of beings that have been attuning the conduct. It corresponds to what *SZ* called "being-in-the-world." Not only does letting-be penetrate the conduct – it "outreaches" it (*vorgreifen*), and reaches up (*umgreifen*) to the attuning totality. The further implication: a given conduct of a human being need not have taken special cognizance of this totality of beings that surrounds all conduct.

> **Thus the conduct of the human being is surrounded by the revealedness of beings in their totality. But this "totality" appears as the incalculable, the unknowable. It cannot be conquered on the basis of such beings as have been revealed already, whether belonging to nature or to history. Though it**

> **is always there around us, it is the indeterminate, the indeterminable. But as such, it is not nothingness – rather it is the concealedness of beings in their totality.** (p. 395)

It is not the conduct but rather the letting-be of *Da-sein* that forms the original relationship of *Da-sein* to the totality of beings. As attuning, the totality was indeed self-revealing, but for the conduct (and perception and speech) it is incalculable and unknowable. Thus, Heidegger is identifying an unconcealment that operates together with our letting-be that is also a concealment, relative to our conduct. The letting-be of beings is the medium in which all conduct is consummated, and it permeates the conduct, but it brings no information. Thus Heidegger can say that the concealment does not arise as some fault in our enumeration of the many things we know: he says (p. 396) that it is "older than" all revealedness of this or that thing, "just as old as letting-be itself." *What Is Metaphysics? (WM)* described the venture of science as breaking into (*Einbruch*) the world totality, but without capturing it in knowledge. The sciences want to know only beings – and nothing else – but they were led nevertheless into a curious relationship to this Nothing, and that became the topic of Heidegger's address. This is the analogy: the totality to which our conduct responds becomes apparent to the conduct (and perception and awareness) as indeterminate and concealed, even as the conduct (and awareness) focus upon this or that entity. All of this is to be understood as the *attunement, Stimmung,* of the conduct by the totality of beings. Thus the totality to which the conduct responds becomes apparent to the conduct (and perception and awareness) as indeterminate and concealed, even as the conduct (and awareness) focus upon this or that entity. We cannot get from that entity to the concealed totality. Thus the concealment does not arise as some fault in our enumeration of the many things we know: it is "older than" all revealedness of this or that thing, "just as old as letting-be itself."

So we need now to inquire into the attuning itself. There is above all an attunement of the human being as such (or of *Da-sein*) by the world totality, that is, by beings as a whole, *das Seiende im Ganzen.* By virtue of this manner of *Gestimmtheit,* every human conduct is "**absorbed into the totality of beings**." What attunes us, Heidegger says, is the totality of the world that is not articulated into separate factors, what "does not coincide with the sum of beings that are actually known." So in *WW* we do not readily discern this attunement, nor that to which the conduct is attuned, nor even that which is becoming attuned – there is in our experience a darkness about all these points. Upon deeper investigation we discover that the attunement is hidden, and moreover that that which attunes is likewise hidden, and that which becomes attuned is hidden. Our study began when somebody encountered a coin and uttered a "truth" about it, and then we proceeded to the deeper conditions for this, especially the speaker's conduct towards the coin, letting it be. Freedom makes beings accessible, and Heidegger can attribute our disclosures and activities to this freedom: it seems to be in command. Yet we shall see that this is not so.

The background for this treatment of attunement, *die Gestimmtheit*, is the study in *SZ*, Section 29, of *die Befindlichkeit*, attunement, or what could also be called affectivity, a central structure pertaining to *Da-sein*'s being-in-the-world. It makes itself evident phenomenally in moods, *Stimmungen.* There attunement was interpreted as a mode of being-in- – which was also an exposure-to- – the world, and others, and things and ourselves. He stresses here a point that was also made in *SZ* 29, that the attunement effected by beings-as-a-whole is one manner in which they are *revealed* – in 1930, it is called their *Offenbarkeit.* In *SZ* attunement stood alongside understanding as a mode of being-in, a mode of disclosure of the world. But here Heidegger stresses a central new point: that this manifestness or revealedness does *not* coincide with our cognition of those entities. As unconcealed, it is also concealed.

For this attunement is *not* phenomenally evident to *Da-sein*, a revision over against *SZ.* He is not forthcoming on his motive for this revision, but we can see that it contributes to his developing argument that the attunement and that which exercises the attunement are radically *concealed.* Quite likely, we can see in this point a rebuke to Max Scheler, whose accounts of emotions and feelings had been mentioned favourably in *SZ.*[75] Heidegger often speaks scornfully of every *Erlebnis* and *erlebende Mensch*, terms that were certainly employed by Scheler. In *WW*, Heidegger holds that the attunements are *not* registered in human consciousness or subjectivity, but rather in *Da-sein*, the essential *grounding* for human consciousness. In *SZ* attunement stood alongside understanding, *Verstehen*, as a mode of being-in, a mode of disclosure of the world. In *SZ* attunement and understanding were "equi-primordial" dimensions of our being-in-the-world. But in *WW*, 1930, the totality to which our conduct responds becomes apparent to the conduct (and perception and awareness) as indeterminate and concealed, even as the conduct (and awareness) focus upon this or that entity. We cannot get from that entity to the concealed totality. All of these negative assertions are moving us more and more closely to the concealment that will shortly become Heidegger's theme.

A key point is that that which has become attuned is, no less than the world as a whole, left in darkness and inexplicitness. Our attunement is not readily discerned in our "experience" (we can certainly think of the responses of the body to its world, though Heidegger does not discuss the body here). We can say that what becomes attuned is not an Ego or a human being, but rather the subterranean *Da-sein* of the human being. Moreover, the theme of attunement offers a corrective to common philosophical ideas of determinism. The long effort in modern science and philosophy to comprehend all conduct as due to causal sequences is set aside here, because the attunement is not due to the actions of certain entities that impact the human being, nor is it due to their joint operation. Rather, it is due to the totality that recedes from the grasp of *Da-sein* and that therefore appears as indeterminate and incalculable.

9. Concealment: Section II(b)(ii) *(1930, pp. 396–8)*

In the Third Arc, concealment was introduced as the concealment of beings as a whole (or concealment of the world), which *Da-sein* endured even while engaging in letting some beings be, and even while being attuned, *gestimmt*, by beings as a whole. It is this and this alone that Heidegger will be treating now, not just any event of concealment (the professor who could not find his umbrella); nor is it an abstract treatment of common features of cases of concealment. Thus, even where this concealment prevails, one is still able to say, truly, "This coin is round" – there is no suggestion of a concealment of such things as that. It is beings as a whole that are concealed, and it is from *Da-sein* that they are concealed.

Now we learn why this concealment is a form of untruth, indeed the pre-eminent form. This is not an obvious point, because it could be argued (and has been, by Tugendhat in his chapter on *WW*[76]) that concealment is, properly speaking, a deprival of information or of knowledge: it embraces what has never been presented to us for our grasping: only when some information is actually apprehended, and therefore not concealed, can one pose the question whether it is true or untrue. Thus the proper opposite to the True is not the Concealed, but the False. Indeed, many of Heidegger's readers, in pondering his earlier references to untruth bonding in some way with truth, might have supposed that it was falsehood he had in mind, falsehood manifested in such phenomena as mistaken perceptions, errors in speech or in understanding the speech of others, primitive explanations of nature, outright lies and deceptions, and so on. In fact, Heidegger will deal with these phenomena in the subsequent units where he presents them as varieties of *die Irre*. His overall argument is that *Irre* is a secondary form of untruth dependent on *Verbergung*. Now we shall show why it is the pre-eminent form of untruth, and also why it takes on the form of mystery, *das Geheimnis*. These units will proceed to show, nevertheless, that concealment (or mystery) pertains intimately and essentially to *truth*. We then we conclude the exposition by treating the everyday life of human beings, showing what traces are seen there of concealment and mystery and how we tend to evade any awareness of it.

Untruth does not merely arise as an unfortunate possibility in our lives; it is found within the essence itself. Here in the 1930 version it is because truth is essential for our own existence – is essential *for us* – that untruth needs to be admitted into the very heart of its essence. When truth is authorized and empowered, when it is a central commitment in our lives (this is the familiar idea of *Wesens-Ermächtigung*), the Non-essence must be admitted into the essence. In this argument, the free human being is the middle term, securing the belonging of the Non-essence to the essence, because of the double scope of freedom. Heidegger already moved beyond the generic concept of untruth to the specific form, concealment (*die Verborgenheit*) by showing that all human conduct is attuned (*gestimmt*). This appeared initially as a kind of unconcealment of things, but a deeper consideration of the matter, as we saw, made it apparent that such attunement is actually a concealment. The attunement does not depend on any awareness we have of such distinct factors; indeed, our very unconsciousness of them is what allows them to work upon us. What attunes us, Heidegger says, is the totality of the world, what is not articulated into separate factors, what "does not coincide with the sum of beings that are actually known."

Now we are to see that concealment does not arise merely as the effect of our conduct, as if our conduct occluded beings as a whole, as if it was afflicted with finitude. It is true that there are texts that could be understood that way, but we see that those texts are corrected, and Heidegger establishes that, on the contrary, concealment is an original power. Heidegger does say, for instance:

> **Precisely where a singular conduct, in relating itself to a being, has let it be and thereby disclosed it, it conceals the beings in their totality. Letting-be is in itself, at the same time, concealment. The freedom of *Dasein* is an existing, disclosing letting-be that also accomplishes, and is, the concealment of beings in their totality. Concealment, that is, non-disclosedness, is untruth in the original sense.** (pp. 395–6)

He does seem to say here that the conduct, in disclosing one thing, is responsible for concealing others, yet he will immediately make it clear that *our agency is not the decisive factor*. The transition to the next paragraph is accomplished smoothly, without any major interruption, yet *this paragraph now assigns an agency to the concealment itself*:

> **The concealment of beings in their totality does not arise as a secondary consequence, as if our survey of the different beings could never be completed, so that we were unable to reveal each and every being. Rather, the concealment of beings in their totality, which is the authentic untruth, is older than all revealedness of this one or that one. It is just as old as letting-be itself that, even as it discloses, also holds in concealment.** (p. 396)

To understand this, we need to think about letting-be in its own relation to concealment. Letting-be is the key function or activity of *Da-sein*, and we remember that it was introduced as the essence of our freedom. We must think of it as thrust out and forward into the opening (into *alētheia*), where it engages in disclosing the world and the many beings. But the power of thrusting out does not itself enter into the light of the *Da*: it withdraws from the open. We must recognize two points: (1) that Heidegger acknowledges that being too, and not just beings, is subject to concealment[77]; and (2) that this also holds for the being of the exister, *das Sein des Da-seins*. Where being is concerned, you cannot make a division between what is out in the world and what works within ourselves. Your own being is hidden. Moreover, the question arises whether the *Sein* of *Seinlassen* falls under concealment as well, for after all the letting-be accomplished by *Da-sein* depends on concealment; as Heidegger says, concealment is "just as old" as letting-be, that is, just as original. Self-concealing is inscribed in its being.

With the revealing letting-be of conduct, penetrated by a concealing of the totality, the totality is present and operates *as* the concealed in all conduct and awareness. The concealment enters in at the start in all awareness, and is not merely the failure of our stock of knowledge to encompass the whole world; it is not a limitation of our cognitive faculty. By contrast with puzzles, this is not a gap in our field of knowledge, whereby some things have not yet been determined while some other things have (certain causes of cancers). Because concealment is just as primordial as unconcealment, and just as primordial as letting-be, it deserves the name of authentic untruth (*eigentliche Unwahrheit*), which is equivalent to "authentic Non-essence of truth." The paragraph we quote continues:

> **And what preserves this letting-be so that it may hold in concealment? Nothing less than the concealment of the totality of the concealed, i.e., mystery. Not one mystery about this or that, but rather the very prevailing of**

> **mystery throughout the Dasein of the human being as such. The letting-be of beings in their totality is at once unveiling and concealing, which brings it about that Dasein is governed through and through by mystery. Insofar as Dasein exists, it is exposed to the primordial and the most extreme non-unveiledness, authentic untruth. The authentic Non-essence of truth is mystery.** (p. 396)

Yet we must take note of another facet of this letting-be, *Seinlassen* – it does not fall completely under concealment, but incorporates a fragmentary relationship to being. While the being of *Da-sein* itself is concealed, the letting-be is revelatory – it discloses beings in the environment as well as being opened up to the totality of beings. It is necessary to remember here some earlier passages in the essay, in which letting-be first made its appearance as Heidegger's interpretation of freedom. Freedom is our opening up to the world; it came to be called the essence of truth because it fulfilled the idea of the Open in which beings came to stand. This freedom also has a major role to play in the later pages that introduce concealment.

Letting-be not only brings about both unconcealment and concealment – it is maintained in that function by the presence of concealment (i.e., its own concealment), which preserves it or guards it in that function. Now the status of concealment is recognized as mystery (*das Geheimnis*). That is because of the union in this untruth of concealment with unconcealment: mystery generally does not merely mean something unknown, but rather something in some way known but that hides its truth and awakens our questing. Our freedom is opened up to the mystery, so that, in a proverb taken from the Chinese *Tao Te Ching* of Lao-Tse, Heidegger can say (pp. 396–7) that the brightness of our consciousness of freedom induces us to hide in the darkness of the mystery.

The complete account of mystery must include a reference to our *forgetting* it. Heidegger repeats well-known points about the human predilection for what is tangible, concrete, ontic, and manageable. But our forgetting the mystery is not on account of our preoccupation with finite things. There is an original turning away from mystery, so that the way it prevails within human life (affecting all our ontic, pragmatic concerns) is in the manner of a forgotten mystery. Just as mystery itself implies a unity of concealment with unconcealment, so the power of mystery is augmented when it is forgotten: "**bestows a special power on that which seemed to be without power because of being forgotten.**" This power induces the final twist in the present coiling pathway. Human beings are not merely oriented towards pragmatic competence – they are so in a special way, a presumptuousness that is based on an obliviousness.

This is the grounding for the in-sistence that marks human ex-sistence, which brings the next twist of untruth, into the "forgotten essence, the un-essential untruth."

This is the conclusion: through our forgetting (turning away from the mystery), the ex-sistent *Da-sein* becomes, instead, in-sistent, and falls into Erring.

10. Erring: Section II(b)(iii) *(1930, pp. 398–9)*

The two divisions of essential untruth, or the Non-essence (*Unwesen*) of truth, are concealment and mystery, on the one hand – older than unconcealedness – and the inauthentic Non-essence that is called erring (*die Irre*). But the two have an essential connection. We have already treated the indifference with which the ordinary human life regards concealment and mystery:

> **[T]he human being can enlarge his Dasein, using all the available requirements, purposes, programmes and manifestoes. He can take its standards from all of that, forgetting beings in their totality. He will take his stand by all these standards, becoming enticed thereby to overvalue himself. Self-important and oblivious, this Dasein will deal with the things it can manage, and gains no access to anything else.** (pp. 397–8)

And so Heidegger draws the conclusion:

> **An oblivious and presumptuous Dasein insists on everything it manages. Ex-sistent, this Dasein is in-sistent. The mystery does still prevail within this insistent existence, but only as the forgotten essence, the essence of truth that has become unessential, or the unessential untruth.** (p. 398)

This second division incorporates that untruth in which the human being actively participates by thought, word, and deed: untruth in human conduct. Heidegger's word for this is *die Irre*, which I translate with the gerund "erring." (Heidegger himself does use the gerund form *das Irren* at several points.) We need to bear in mind that if erring qualifies human conduct or behaviour, it does not mainly apply to opinions or judgments, so that "error" (the usual meaning of *der Irrtum*) is not the main subject of analysis here: as Heidegger explains, it is something derivative. The term *Irre* is one of those German words that come from the Latin – here the source word is *errare*, to wander astray, which is for Heidegger a permanent kind of movement in *Dasein* from which he will be deriving a whole group of phenomena:

> **What one generally, and in philosophy, recognizes as error, falsehood in judgments, is only one form of erring and a superficial form at that.** (pp. 398–9)

This comes across quite clearly in German, because the colloquial concrete sense of *die Irre* is "madwoman" (its masculine equivalent *der Irre* means "crazyman"); contemporary parlance usually features the plural – on the Autobahn, drivers always exclaim *Sie fahren wie die Irren!* "These drivers are crazy!" So in this chapter Heidegger is ascribing a kind of craziness to us all.

Erring is that untruth that human beings commit when they have forgotten the mystery. Earlier Heidegger was not speaking of a specific mystery, or mysteries, but had in mind the general circumstance that mystery pervades human existence. If mystery is a concealedness that reaches us, of which we are aware, we can recognize that to be aware of a mystery is to know that something is unknown, that it withdraws. So we must now explore what it means for a mystery to be *forgotten* – or, we may say, *repressed* (*verdrängt*). Heidegger says the mystery does not lose its power thereby but becomes present, or potent, in another way. In this situation, freed from mystery, we confine ourselves to whatever is accessible, knowable and fixable. We now possess a confidence that everything is at hand and manageable, and that we in particular are completely in command of ourselves. I act and think as if I myself had established the measures by which I measure my life, which is never the case. Here lies the power of the forgetting of the mystery. In a mode of life constructed on a forgetting, we believe that we have established a goal for ourselves: it could be property, wealth, family, love, sex, rewards, titles, power, fame, pleasure, freedom, community, nation, *Volk*, knowledge, competence, skill – and the character of our consciousness is a confusion in that we believe we have established the goal with our autonomous reason when in fact it is established and assigned to us by some ruling portion of humanity. This essential confusion in every life is what leads us to insist on our goals with a special egotism. I am in-sistent on my goal because it is for me a marker of my identity, and it would not be worthy of me to have received my identity from the general culture. What Heidegger calls here "in-sistence" could also be called obsession: I am determined (*beharrt*) to stand on the values that form my identity; I insist stubbornly (*versteifend*) on my "choices," asserting both that they are "self-evident" and yet that they constitute my *peculiar* merit. Heidegger is ready to call this posture not only our blundering (*Sich-versehen*) but our presumptuousness (*Sich-vermessen*); he explains that in this posture human beings make themselves the "subject," the "standard" for all beings. Thus we have often seen that the "man of property" can understand his property as proving that he is really quite clever, indeed rational and wise, and he may suppose that the propertyless are on the whole incapable and unsound. The scholar of considerable learning may suppose himself to be a summit of mankind, armed against all others with wisecracks and put-downs.

We saw that, through our forgetting (turning away from the mystery), the ex-sistent *Da-sein* has become in-sistent. This means a turning to Erring, another Corner that introduces this second form of untruth. From the conjunction of error and freedom will arise Necessity (p. 399), which is the complete Non-essence of truth.

But the confusion of human life also appears in the fact that the values people call fundamental and self-evident are wobbly and unstable. *Da-sein* inclines away (*wendet*) from the mystery just as it inclines towards everything that is manageable – a turning that happens all at once. This implies a character of motion in *Da-sein* that Heidegger calls a To-and-Fro (*Hin und Her*). Heidegger does not speak of thrownness or falling in this paragraph (the terminology from *SZ*) but rather of turning (*die Wende*), and this is an unstable posture, a turning to and fro. In its dynamic, *Da-sein* moves always on to yet another goal, yet another prize:

> **Human beings go astray. Human beings stray into error, and cannot leave that path because they exist insistently, i.e., because from the start they have already been astray. It belongs to the inner constitution of *Dasein* itself to go astray. Their wandering astray opens up the scope for the turning in which an insistent existence revolves, ceaselessly forgetting itself in unending presumption.** (p. 398)

Throughout our life, we progress from one purpose or goal to an array of others without reflecting on this perpetual change. It is not possible for human value-setting to remain satisfied by one preference or one prize. Turned away from mystery, we enter a *plurality*. And Heidegger presents these inconstant choices as a form of drivenness or passivity, an *Umgetriebenheit.* That gives us the completed sense of *Irre*: we are made to lurch from one thing to another throughout our life. All our worldly preoccupation, managing and controlling, can be understood as going further and further astray: this managing is seen by Heidegger as a *passive* state: being chased, *Umgetriebenheit,* from one item of business to another, and another.

Through our forgetting (turning away from the mystery), the ex-sistent *Da-sein* has become in-sistent, entering into erring, the second form of untruth, characterized by the unstable wandering. To use the terms in which we have characterized the whole text, this is another Corner, the transition from concealment to erring:

> **The Non-essence of truth can become unessential, and this is authentic untruth, i.e., the mystery. But inauthentic untruth comes to constitute itself in its essence by distancing itself from the mystery – and that is erring. And erring is the ground of the possibility of error. By the latter we understand the many possible ways of being mistaken: making mistakes, blundering, going astray, climbing too high, losing one's way, and so on – miscalculation in the widest and decisive sense, by which Dasein can miscalculate and go astray. What one generally and in philosophy recognizes as error, falsehood in judgments, is only one form of erring, and a superficial form at that.** (p. 398)

Die Irre is now shown to yield a whole cornucopia of varying forms: the first offspring mentioned is error (*Irrtum*), which then takes on further modifications, a variety only suggested, not completely enumerated here, making mistakes (*Sich-vertun*) and several other varieties. The common origin of them all is human presumption, our mistaken self-assessment, *Sich-Vermessen,* due to oblivion of the mystery. Perhaps the main interest of this paragraph is the remark in which Heidegger accuses philosophy of having confined its attention to one relatively late offspring of *Irre,* namely, falsehood in judgments, *die Falschheit des Urteils.* We saw earlier that the truth of statements arose out of the truth of conduct (and we saw the background of that doctrine in *SZ,* Section 33, on the statement and conduct). Here is the equivalent point that false judgments should be an offshoot of getting lost, blundering, and other forms of an *existence* gone astray.

Nevertheless, we have to note that in turning away from mystery, and in cultivating only what can be managed and manipulated, the initial essence of truth is still present, because this in-sistent form of existence continues to discern and allow directives from the things it is managing. It is still ek-sistent. It still takes its standards from them and from their binding force. Erring, or wandering astray, would not be possible without this. But this posture is turned away not only from the world-whole that has become concealed, but also from itself and from its existence.

As with someone who is crazy, we are not aware of our condition, and Heidegger means to attribute it to us all (including himself!). It is an original perversity belonging to the human condition, expressing the fate that is given with our being. Thus erring is not like the unhappy mistakes that arise from some turn of events in the world (when ice looks like water on the road) – it is not contingent or accidental mistakes. *Die*

Irre means straying or wandering, and the origin of it is the first straying, our turning away from mystery. The question will arise: if this is a claim covering everyone, on what grounds can Heidegger defend it? Indeed, if all errant human beings are not aware of their condition, what can have permitted Heidegger to assert this strong claim in the first place? It will be vital to grasp the answer to this problem – I shall return to it at the end of the exposition.

Let us use the main previous points to guide us as to the primordial essence of truth: the essence of truth reveals itself as freedom. The latter is ek-sistent, disclosive, letting beings be. On page 399, Heidegger now manoeuvres a further Corner in the coiling pathway that will then be further elaborated in the two concluding paragraphs of the section. We have seen that erring pertains to the inner constitution of *Dasein* itself – it is in the *Dasein* of the human being and misleads him. Yet here the inquiry makes a surprising turn:

> **And yet, as misleading, this erring contributes to the possibility that the human being has of not allowing himself to be misled, i.e., not to overlook himself in the mystery of *Dasein*.** (p. 399)

This is also followed up. Human erring or straying can, after all, come into a connection with the forgotten mystery, so that the two forms of untruth become united, and their interaction is highlighted in this paragraph. The human being is oppressed through the constancy of erring, yet in that oppression there is a possible contact with the mystery. The reference here to necessity is accompanied by a word-play that we cannot translate – we are turning (*Wende*) in our plight (*Not*), to yield necessity (*Notwendigkeit*). But the thought that underlies the words is accessible: through the combined force of mystery and erring, the human being discovers something essential about the structure of the world, discovers a necessity – this arises through the very compulsion or necessity that we experience. We are drawing an unexpected consequence from the principle that Heidegger has been highlighting again and again in the essay: that the complete essence of truth must include its non-essence, both forms of the non-essence. This is the beginning of the ending of the text, for it will make a derivation of *philosophy* from the character of the human predicament. That is highlighted by the most important statements of this paragraph:

> **It is only through its binding itself by that essence that is most intimate to it, and to which it bears a native affinity, that the liberation of Dasein can occur. The full essence of truth is the freedom that makes necessity of itself: the freedom that, as existent, lets be the beings as such and in their**

> **totality. This letting-be comes to pass properly through being opened up to the mystery, which also means through a struggle against being misled by erring. To err while being open to the mystery of beings in their totality means questioning beings in their totality, i.e., to ask what beings are as such. To ask what they are means to seek after the being of beings as such and in their totality. This questioning is what has long been called philosophizing. The liberation of the human being for existence, in word and deed, takes place as philosophizing.** (p. 400)

We have been reminded that the essence of truth must *include* the non-essence of truth rather than excluding it (or excluding both of the forms of it that we have encountered). This point now takes on a new, surprising relevance: if we continue to probe the essence of truth as the freedom that brings unconcealedness, we discover that erring and the mystery are contained within that essence. It is this essence that keeps the human being, or *Da-sein*, in the condition of being needy. What is it then that is recuperated by the power of the essence at work within the non-essence? It is philosophy. Philosophy arises in a situation of being needy or bereft (*die Not*) in which there can arise the consciousness of having wandered astray and continuing to err.

Therewith we can answer the question that arose earlier: we asked how Heidegger could claim to know about an erring that supposedly afflicts all human beings (including himself!), when it was a part of the phenomenon of erring, as with craziness, that one does not know one has it. The answer is that, like all the rest of *WW*, that analysis was the work of philosophy, the ultimate form of truth that we have now shown in its derivation.

Only in the most general terms does *WW* indicate how *die Irre* brings forth the many kinds of untruth that lie in its kingdom: making mistakes, confusion, and, in particular, the one that has mainly preoccupied philosophers: *der Irrtum*, falsity of opinion or judgment. Yet in his lectures on Plato, **31–32** and **33–34**, Heidegger will spend a great deal of effort in showing (a) how untruth belongs essentially to truth, and (b) how Plato and the Greeks treated the different kinds of untruth, and false opinion in particular. We treat his lectures on untruth in the *Theaetetus* at the end of Unit 11 of Part II.

11. The End of the Pathway

(A) From Erring to Philosophy: A Fourth Arc (1930, pp. 400–1)

The derivation of philosophy is from the combination of mystery and erring, that is, from the possibility of *Dasein*, embedded in erring, becoming open to the prevailing of mystery as such. In this paragraph the conclusion drawn is that erring opens us up to truth in the form of philosophy. Philosophy only comes to pass out of the life of human beings who are oppressed by erring. The glimpse into the mystery out of erring is a questioning – in the sense of that unique question of what beings as such are as a whole. The unity of mystery and erring can also be redescribed, I think, as the union of necessity and freedom. We have already treated freedom at length in our earlier meditation on the experience of accepting a binding force, whereby our conduct prepared the way for truth. Freedom was the openness towards that which binds us. Through the coiling pathway of the essence, this freedom was led into its deeper essence: letting-be, which is the letting-be of beings, of what-is. But because letting-be is guided by an understanding of being, the free agent is perforce led to the *question,* "What are beings as such and in their totality?" In this exercise of freedom, the agent is now open to being bound by the being of beings, by the essence of being, and that is what is necessary. Heidegger can call this openness to being bound by being the liberation of the human being. This is philosophizing, and it is the last of the permutations of truth.

The address concludes by returning to the opposition that dominated the Introduction to the address, between philosophy and common sense. We now know from the studies of the Non-essence of truth that common sense ignores and forgets every mystery; we have read in the immediately preceding passage that mystery has had its share in the shaping of philosophy. The speaker of 1930 highlights their contrast: common sense has its easy-going habits, and it wants a doctrine that will be useful to the public – but philosophy refuses all such accommodation. He introduces philosophy in terms that recall its origins in Greek antiquity, especially Heraclitus and Parmenides:

> **This letting-be comes to pass properly through being opened up to the mystery, which also means through a struggle against being misled by erring. To err while being open to the mystery of beings in their totality means questioning beings in their totality, i.e., to ask what beings are as such. To ask what they are means to seek after the being of beings as such and in their totality. This questioning is what has long been called philosophizing.** (p. 400)

We may think of the openness of Heraclitus to mystery ("Nature loves to hide," no. 123) at the same time as his constant preoccupation with erring in thought and in life ("Human nature has no power of understanding, but the divine nature has it," no. 78; see also nos. 1, 17, 34, 51

56). It is precisely the combination of these two forms of the essence of untruth that accounts for the genesis of philosophy. Parmenides, too, was greeted by his goddess in an atmosphere of mystery, and haunted by erring: " No evil fate has dispatched thee on thy journey by this road (for truly it is far from the path trodden by mankind); no it is divine command and Right" (quoting from the first fragment). Heidegger proceeds next to link the emergence of philosophy to a recognition of necessity, as a counterweight to freedom; and this too can be documented from the very earliest philosophers – we think of Heraclitus again with his doctrine of the *logos* that stands opposed to the varying whims of the majority of humankind ("Though all things come into being in accordance with this *logos*, men seem as if they had never met with it," no. 1; see also nos. 2, 30, 50, 94.). We may think as well of the entire message of Parmenides: "powerful Necessity holds it is the bonds of a Limit, which constrains it round about, because it is decreed by divine law that Being should not be without boundary" (quoting from Fragment 8). For Heidegger, however, necessity is not merely opposed to freedom – it also *infuses* freedom, just in the way in which the essence of untruth informs the essence of truth.

But philosophy does not mingle with, or make compromise with, common sense – it wages an unending polemic against it. The constitution of philosophy differs from common sense in being marked by a duality or discordance (*Zwiespalt*) owing to its openness to mystery. On the one hand, it has a gentleness and a releasement (*Gelassenheit der Milde)* through being open to mystery and concealment, unlike common sense. We can interpret this as the gentleness of philosophical dialogue that is rooted in its contemplative essence, its knowing about its own un-knowing. On the other hand, philosophy has a hardness or rigour (*Strenge*) in forcing its question upon beings, forcing them to declare what they are, a rigour that is foreign to common sense. The duality that defines philosophy (and surely it is his own philosophy that Heidegger is thinking of) bestows on it a character very much like Kant's, to be confirmed through a Kant quotation that brings the address to an end. In 1930, Kant was still, as he had been through the late 1920s, Heidegger's philosophical ideal. In analysing the quotation, we may ask where in Kant we can find something like Heidegger's duality.

The quotation is from the *Grounding for the Metaphysics of Morals*,[78] the Second Section, "Transition from Popular Moral Philosophy to a Metaphysics of Morals."

Here philosophy is seen in fact to be put in a precarious position, which should be firm even though there is neither in heaven nor on earth anything on which it depends or is based. Here philosophy must show its purity as

author of its laws, and not as the herald of such laws as are whispered to it by an implanted sense or by who knows what tutelary nature.

At this point in his argument, Kant is renouncing emphatically any grounding of morality through empirical usefulness, religion, humankind's natural conditions, or any such factors that Kant considers to be extraneous. Only a completely a priori reason is competent to provide a foundation: morality will be a law prescribed by reason, not an axiom of prudence. The authority of the law is strengthened indeed, the fewer subjective causes or auxiliary motivations that are adduced. Philosophy speaks for this a priori reason, and will proceed to establish on the basis of the a priori moral law a metaphysics of morals – its content includes the very idea of humanity as an end in itself, the doctrine of freedom, and the autonomy of the moral agent as the supreme principle of morality. Heidegger's present argument on behalf of philosophy shares with Kant's a stern separation of philosophy from every interest represented by common sense and social advantage, a purity in its concentration upon being, and truth, that is his counterpart to the metaphysics of morals. Kant's reason also stands in a duality or *Zwiefalt* because it must determine its objects thoroughly – especially the laws of reason – but receives no help from the noumenal world, which is, in effect, a mystery.

We may note that Heidegger had just concluded his 1930 Summer Semester lecture course, "The Essence of Human Freedom" (*GA* 31) with this very same Kant quotation. The second half of the course had been an exploration of the Kantian account of causality (drawing especially on the "Second Analogy") and a correlation of that doctrine with the account of freedom found in the First Critique (especially the "Third Antinomy") and in the Second Critique. Following Kant's doctrine of the primacy of practical reason over the theoretical, Heidegger argues that causality can be rooted back in the transcendental freedom of subjectivity, that is, that causality is rooted in freedom, not freedom in causality. That conclusion is stated explicitly in the final page of the lecture course (*GA* 31, p. 303). Against that background, his concluding quotation gains a tremendous force: philosophy and freedom take on a universal, ontological autonomy.

(B) Philosophy and the Academic Disciplines

This reading of Kant was prepared by several earlier studies of Kant that embodied an extremely strong focus on the a priori character of knowledge, with an accompanying strong emphasis on philosophy as the agent of that knowledge. Philosophy is given a supremacy over science in the doctrines of the 1929 "Kant book," *Kant and the Problem of Metaphysics.*[79] While a given science affords us knowledge of a certain range of entities, there is a prior ontological knowledge on which it depends, the regional ontology that delineates what character an entity must have to belong to this region or that – for example, to be an object of physics, the entity needs to be a part of nature, and not, say, of history or spirit. But that regional ontology itself needs to be correlated with the entire understanding of being that is the territory of philosophy. Thus we read:

> **Knowledge of beings is only possible on the grounds of a prior knowledge, free of experience, of the constitution of the being of beings.** (p. 36)

This supremacy of philosophy over science is the echo of a point Heidegger had made in study after study in the 1920s: the supremacy of *truth* over science. In his earliest days he had not held such a view. We may look to the example of Heinrich Rickert, Heidegger's dissertation adviser. For Rickert, science was not defined merely as the grasp of the things that are – it took the form of judgments, which involve a claim of validity, *Geltung*, expressed in universal assertions that we grounded in evidence. Thus the object of a cognitive or scientific judgment is not merely that which exists, but the ideal of truth towards which it is always moving. Science finds its fulfilment in that ideal or value that we call truth.

The young Heidegger absorbed very well the lessons of neo-Kantianism. He gave a lecture in 1915 to qualify for an academic post, where he worked out the differences between physical sciences and historical science with respect to the distinct concepts of time employed by them both. In his introductory remarks he offers the following characterization of science in general, entirely in accord with Rickert:

> **If we understand science according to the idea of its completeness, then we see it as a self-sufficient network of meaning that holds, *geltenden Sinnes.* But the separate concrete sciences that have grown up historically as cultural formations are never completed – they always on the way towards discovering truth.**[80]

But in the years to come, Heidegger not only moved beyond neo-Kantianism into his own variant of phenomenology – he did so in a way that completely overturned the relationship between truth and science. Where once he had recognized that science had instituted truth, he now maintains that truth brings forth science. Where the tradition thought of truth-values as assigned to statements or judgments, Heidegger finds that truth is more widely disseminated in every form of experience and that it has only a contingent connection with logic, science, and the theory of knowledge. *But for the phenomenologist, the domain of truth is coextensive with that of philosophy!* We may quote many documents of the 1920s to that effect.

In *GA 21*, the Logic lectures, we see Heidegger's effort to overturn the typical academic views of his time, reviewing the theory of knowledge that had predominated in Germany during his youth. Rickert is reviewed on pages 83 to 85. The phenomenologist of the 1920s expressed a very specific view of the relation between science and truth, making the former dependent on the latter. Let us quote some brief statements from the 1927 *Phenomenology and Theology*:

> **Science is the founding disclosure, for the sheer sake of disclosure, of a self-contained region of beings, or of being. Every region of objects, according to its subject matter and the mode of being of its objects, has its own mode of possible disclosure, evidence, founding, and its own conceptual formation of the knowledge thus arising ... Ontic sciences in each case thematize a given being that in a certain manner is always already disclosed *prior* to scientific discovery[81] ... [A] being that in some way is already disclosed is to a certain extent come upon as a possible theme of theoretical objectification and inquiry ... [T]his given positum is come upon in a definite prescientific manner of approaching and proceeding with that being.[82]**

This relation of science and truth is confirmed as well by *SZ*. Sections 12 and 13 analyse the being of *Da-sein* as being-in-the-world. The important inference is drawn that our knowledge of the world is secondary to our being-in-the-world, a function of it. Then Section 44 propounds a phenomenological account of truth that shows how our interpretations and statements accomplish an uncovering (*Entdecken*) of their objects. Then Heidegger traces the event of uncovering, that is, truth, in all kinds of experiences of *Da-sein*, from uttering statements to practical conduct, and shows the wider expression of truth in the disclosedness of *Da-sein*'s being in the world as a whole. A bit further on in the book, Section 69, Heidegger makes a kind of deduction: the sciences emerge through a revolution in *Da-sein*'s understanding of being, by means of "the mathematical projection of nature." This derivation does not in any manner impugn the truth of science, but shows that this projection has brought a narrowing and compartmentalizing of truth.

We may look at the lectures on Kant of 1927–28.[83] Section 2 shows in detail how the correlation of science and pre-scientific experience is actually carried out. Science is not our first mode of dwelling in the world, but it is developed from the more primordial possibility given with human existence, the possibility of knowing things in the world. We take the step into scientific understanding when we engage in objectifying things (*Vergegenständlichung*). It is for phenomenology to trace these different postures and correlate each of them with one or another variant of truth. In science, we engage in unveiling precisely and solely for the purpose of unveiling, and this brings a revolution (*Umstellung*) in our way of being-in-the-world.

We shall add some lines from the 1929 "On the Essence of Ground" that apply the phenomenology of science and experience directly to the question of truth:

> **[B]eings as the concern of any predicative determination, must already be manifest *before* such predication and *for* it. For it to be possible, predication must be able to take up residence in a making-manifest that is *not predicative* in character. Propositional truth is rooted in a *more originary* truth (unconcealment), in the pre-predicative manifestness *of beings*, which may be called *ontic truth.*[84]**

Things of the world are of different kinds, and the manifestness or unconcealment they exhibit will vary accordingly: inert objects will be at best (as he says) uncovered, whereas we ourselves, human beings, have a very distinct and primordial openness. To these and other differences correspond most of the variations of our distinct discourses (physics, biology, history, interpersonal communication, poetry, religion, and so on):

> **In keeping with the different kinds and domains of beings, the character of their possible manifestness and of the accompanying ways of interpretively determining them changes. Thus, for example, the truth of what is present at hand (for example[,] material things) as discoveredness is specifically distinct from the truth of those beings that we ourselves are, from the disclosedness of existing *Da-sein.*[85]**

The differences in the mode of being of what pertains to nature, and what pertains to history, lead into deeper reflections on being. So here science must yield to philosophy:

> **The fundamental concepts of contemporary science neither contain the "proper" ontological concepts of the being of those beings concerned, nor can such concepts be attained merely through a "suitable" extension of**

> **these fundamental concepts. Rather, the originary ontological concepts must be attained *prior* to any scientific definition of fundamental concepts. For it is from those ontological concepts that it first becomes possible to assess the restrictive way – which in each case delimits from a particular perspective – in which the fundamental concepts of the sciences correlate with being, which can be grasped in these purely ontological concepts.**[86]

He concludes this argument with the remark that what gives grounding to the beings of nature, history, and other regions is a deeper doctrine of truth than that of predication:

> **Our task hitherto has merely been to show, in a few essential steps, that the essence of truth must be sought more originarily than the traditional characterization of truth in the sense of a property of assertions would admit.**[87]

Thus the differences in the sciences and other forms of discourse actually spring from different forms of truth. So Heidegger never adopted the view or prejudice that scientific knowledge was the privileged home of truth. Truth appears more widely. In these citations, we have been inquiring how Heidegger was capable of making truth his topic in advance of any theory of science or knowledge.

The trajectory of Heidegger's work during the 1920s, up to 1930, is therefore an almost unprecedented defence of philosophy as the supreme form of knowledge, thematizing truth and being in its utterly autonomous way (recalling the quote from Kant's ethics). The main course of this trajectory did not emphasize any character of mystery, so in this respect what we read at the end of the *WW* address is quite new and did not become fully effective in Heidegger's thought in the early 1930s. It was the insistent driving force that we see in "On the Essence of Ground" that set the tone for the immediate future. Philosophy is the a priori that sets the conditions for each science with its characteristic themes of being and truth. That permits the sciences to discover their own "truths" about the beings they investigate. Here and elsewhere through the 1930s Heidegger tended to speak of philosophy as a body of ontological knowledge rather than the experience of questioning or the encounter with mystery. We have just seen how philosophy offers directives to the other forms of knowledge – scientific, empirical – in a way that is close to the role of a philosopher-king. It is for us now to see the consequences. It turned out that assigning a guiding role of this sort to philosophy had the most drastic consequences. For this was translated into an institutional, administrative context. It became the prototype for Heidegger's claim, in 1933, that he ought to be the Führer of the German universities.

INTERMISSION

Political Storms

Our opening section on Heidegger's Introduction concluded with the question how truth in mathematics depends upon the essence of truth. Such a question can be repeated with respect to physics, chemistry, biology, and all other disciplines. If we *were* able to answer such questions, we might be able to see how the many disciplines of the university could become integrated and the scholars form a true community, under the benevolent gaze of a philosopher. There is little doubt, looking at Heidegger's courses in this period, that he intended to pursue just this problem: *GA* 29–30, for instance, devotes a great deal of attention to biology and the concomitant problems of the philosophy of life.

But it was just after Heidegger's return to Freiburg that Germany and the world entered a new period of crisis. The ominous changes in the world were registered more strongly, perhaps, in Germany than anywhere else. The Great Depression began with bank failures on the Continent, and in Germany, industry and commerce began to shrink; food supplies were threatened; unemployment in Germany mounted until in 1932 it reached 7 million; there was widespread starvation. As successive governments stewed between 1929 and 1932, the population experienced a radicalizing and polarizing of political opinions. There were armed confrontations on the streets; the Communist Party overtook the SPD; nationalist and military voices tended to drown out the liberal and "bourgeois" parties; many deserted the older parties of the Right and Centre to join the National Socialists under Hitler, who realized increasing gains election after election.

In September 1930, the Nazis had their "breakthrough" election: they attracted more than 6 million votes as against 800,000 in the previous election, so that their representation in the Reichstag increased eightfold; with 107 seats, they were now in second place after the SPD. In the election of July 1932, they more than doubled their seats again, to 230;

the voters' turnout had increased by 4 million, largely due to a huge surge of young voters. The Nazis were now the largest party in the Reichstag. Their seat count fell slightly in November 1932, but in January 1933 they were able to form a government, and with support from the "Conservatives" of von Hugenberg, they had over 50 per cent of the vote in Germany's last election in March 1933. And Heidegger joined in: he supported the National Socialist party. This option for Nazism was not really determined by any philosophical factors; it was mainly determined by his appraisal of the current circumstances of Germany. Here I stray into the domain of history and biography and can only express my judgment on the basis of what I have read myself. In the essay "Heidegger, Nietzsche and Politics,"[88] Otto Pöggeler quotes from a notebook of Hermann Mörchen, Heidegger's student, after a visit with Heidegger at the end of 1931:

> Heidegger and his wife had become National Socialists. "He does not understand much about politics. And therefore it was especially his disdain for mediocrity and for doing things by half measures that made him expect something from the Party, which had promised to do something decisive and to contradict communism effectively."

The question of his choice is not answered by philosophical analysis – it is not that there is a continuing slide from the fundamental ontology to the politics. The explanations for Hitler's appeal that historians have offered (Kershaw, Bullock, Ferguson, Winkler) are well-suited to the particular case of Heidegger as well. Near the beginning of the *Spiegel* interview (published posthumously in May 1976), Heidegger describes his motivations during the winter of 1932–33:

> **My neighbor, Professor von Möllendorf was chosen Rector. The installation of the new Rector here takes place on April 15. During the winter semester of 1932–33, we discussed the [current] situation often, not only the political one, but especially that of the universities and the partially hopeless situation of the students. My judgment went like this: to the extent that I can judge things, the only possibility still available [to us] is to try to seize upon the approaching developments with those constructive forces that still remain alive.**[89]

My quotations from Mörchen and the *Spiegel* interview (to be sure, only tiny bits of evidence from an immense mass full of conflict) lead me to focus on the awareness that a citizen has of the state of his country, economic, political, and otherwise. As Mörchen says, Heidegger had minimal talent in political analysis, of course, but I suppose his millions of contemporaries were not much wiser. I am saying that Martin and Elfride Heidegger were carried along by a popular wave, motivated by the appalling circumstances of Germany at the time. The thinker who will want to be the leader of university renewal in 1933 was really just a follower in politics in 1931. I have tried to show something common and pedestrian in this matter to make more comprehensible the choice that Citizen Heidegger made. But it had major consequences.

In April 1933, Freiburg University needed a new rector, and – by a confusing, controversial process that has been much studied[90] – Heidegger was installed in the office. The process needs no comment from me; my concern is what he said and did as Rector, and whether and how it reflects on his philosophy. In all his later comments (*Spiegel*; *Facts and Thoughts*), he says that his goal in assuming the rectorate was to realize the program that he had announced in the 1929 *WM*. We may, then, analyse his 1933 address upon assuming the rectorate, "The Self-assertion of the German University"[91] (*SU*), to see what elements do come from 1929 and what new elements may have entered his thought, presumably from the political conjuncture.

The address affirms the correlation that *WM* established between the university and our devotion to *Wissenschaft*. The essence of the university is not the organization it acquired over past centuries, or its mode of governance (*SU*, nos. 2, 4), but the will to *Wissenschaft* that informs the life of the teachers and students (*SU*, nos. 6, 8). And much of the description of *Wissenschaft* repeats *WM*: in *WM*, he said that *Wissenschaft* is the irruption, *Einbruch*, of the human being into the whole of beings, breaking them open so that they can show what and how they are. That is repeated here: *Wissenschaft* began in Greece "**when Western man stands up for the first time ... and faces beings taken as a whole and grasps them as those beings which they are**" (*SU*, no. 9). *But* now in 1933, Heidegger puts the university into service for the people: "**to educate and discipline the leaders and guardians of the fate of *das deutsche Volk***" (*SU*, no. 6). And so, from the title of his address consistently through to the end, Heidegger's theme is the *German* university. At the climax of the address (*SU*, nos. 22–5), Heidegger announces the three forms of service that the German student body owes to the people: labour, bearing arms, and study. To that end, the traditional academic freedom of the student body must be abandoned. One would not have foreseen these demands in 1929.

In another echo of 1929, Heidegger remains preoccupied with the estrangement of academic faculties and disciplines from one another, claiming that, with the rediscovery of the grounding for *Wissenschaft*, the university can recover its communal essence: "**Such questioning shatters the division of the sciences into rigidly separately specialties, carries them back from their endless and aimless dispersal into isolated fields and corners**" (*SU*, no. 19). As in 1929, the renewal of the whole community and the exploration of the grounding of *Wissenschaft* is specifically the work of philosophers. There was some recognition in 1929 of the ancient Greek discovery of philosophy, but that is given much more weight in 1933. Amid all the Greek questions here, Heidegger believes that the philosopher in modern times can also hearken to the message of the ancients, the "remote decree," *die ferne Verfügung*, by which the vocation of philosophy reaches into the present by way of the future, though stemming from the past (*SU*, nos. 14–16). The grounding of *Wissenschaft* was also its beginning.

This is connected to another aspect of *SU* that has no precedent at all in 1929. Able to follow the remote decree, Heidegger as philosopher and now rector is also the Führer of the university. This represents the sharpest incursion of National Socialism into the university. The speech begins with the assertion of his supremacy, and he will call the student body and the teaching staff his retinue, *Gefolgschaft*. At a lower level, though, the professors are also the Führer of the students, and it is the destiny of the students to take their place, in the professions, as Führer within the *Volk*. One expression of the rector's function as Führer is to provide the philosophical concept of knowledge (*SU*, no. 30) – it is "**to seize and give new form to the basic ways in which teachers and students work knowledgeably together in faculties and specializations.**" What then is this essence of knowledge that the rector defines for his community? It has a twofold composition: first, it is a questioning endurance amid the uncertainty of beings as a whole (*SU*, nos. 6, 13, 20); second, it is the destiny of the German people giving form to that exposure. The second provision is of course quite new in 1933, but the first component is closely related to the atmosphere of the 1929 address, which emphasized the revelatory power of anxiety that thrusts us before an estranged, unintelligible world. This is developed in 1933 into an almost paranoid vision of the "**hard-pressing insistence**" and the "**unfathomable constancy**" of all things (*SU*, nos. 12, 21), the "**utterly unprotected exposure to what is concealed and uncertain**" (*SU*, no. 18). In such a world and such a university, the teachers and students can expect no rest or serenity, but must employ their strength in a continuing effort of struggle (*Kampf*). One can well understand that Heidegger's earlier disposition of anxiety has found here a new and activist resolution. *Wissenschaft* is realized in questioning; and in confronting dubious answers, as "the cognitive struggle of questioners" (*SU*, no. 38).

What is perhaps the central theme of *SU*, linking its pedagogical interest to its political goals, is the intimate link it proposes between the rector's *Führerschaft* and the needs of the German people. The thrust of its opening lines is that a rector can claim to be a leader of the university only if he is led by "**the relentlessness of the spiritual mission that impels the destiny of the German people**." The people of course require leaders and guardians who will come from the university, but most of all the *geistige Welt* of the people is what gives them greatness, endurance, turbulence, and a future – and this is the spiritual and intellectual world that is built and kept for them by their universities (*SU*, no. 20). But Heidegger thought that now in 1932 and 1933 the people had revealed itself, it had chosen itself, and undertaken to march into the future. He thought that he understood this great event. The rectoral address is explicit in welcoming the new regime in Germany, and in proclaiming that universities have to be brought into line with it. The rector will be attempting some coercive reforms, not just in matters of governance (that would be too superficial) but in the very conduct of study and teaching. And here we must ask how Heidegger understands these deeper matters. Yes, there is now a National Socialist party in power in Berlin and the provinces, with its hierarchy reaching up to Hitler the Führer, but what matters to Heidegger is something else – National Socialism is a *movement* of the people, whose most valuable aspect is the youth movement.[92] The movement emerges from the *Volksgemeinschaft* (*SU*, no. 23) – it is a breakthrough, *Aufbruch* (*SU*, nos. 45, 46) that now confronts the further task of building itself up. The speech opens by referring to the German people with their special destiny, *Schicksal* – to march into the future. Now the rector claims to have some special affinity with this movement in *Aufbruch: it* is the source of his authority, not the organization of the party. *The movement of the people is the grounding and essence of the party, and provides for the philosopher the guarantee of his vision of the grounding and essence of knowledge, truth, and the university.*

Only because of this "populist" claim that he had special access to the essential wishes of the people could Heidegger attempt his coercive reform of the university. But we can see now, and within about a year he himself was able to see, that this "special access" was an illusion. That was his essential mistake in politics – it was not any cynical pandering to the upper echelons of the Nazi Party.

Though this story has become well known, not everybody has been able to distinguish the two elements that are interwoven in it:

(a) Heidegger's work in the 1920s culminated in the view that philosophy's mission was to investigate the a priori, the ontological conditions for every science, with ontological truth determining every ontic truth. And now this relationship between philosophy and science is to receive institutional recognition, with philosophy recognized in its *Führerschaft* within the university.

(b) But Heidegger is also assimilating this institutional structure to the specific political conjuncture of 1933 Germany: the National Socialist seizure of power. This setting was not something he invented; indeed there is no reason to think he had even anticipated it before 1930. But he was ready to accommodate his intellectual views and his institutional ambition to what he saw as the prevailing reality because (unlike some intellectuals) he actually welcomed the Nazi seizure of power.

In Part II of this study we shall document the changes whereby he left behind both points (a) and (b). Though there is ample evidence that he came to regret this choice,[93] he never made public acknowledgments of guilt of the sort that would placate his critics.

What then should one say? What led Heidegger into Nazism in the first place? I think we do not find the explanation in any of the 1920s work, or in the practice of thinking we have been tracing in 1930. His political choice was determined by his appraisal of the current circumstances of Germany. But none of this (e.g., his own preference in voting for Hitler) would have had such disastrous effects if Heidegger had not yielded to the temptation to assume the office of Rector of Freiburg University – installed as the Führer of the university, he issued intemperate encyclicals in support of Hitler, hints of which we can see in his **33–34** Plato course, until he burned himself out and resigned in the spring of 1934. This mismatch between the man and the office has the character of tragedy.

The Winter Semester of 1933–34 represents the peak of Heidegger's political engagement. During this semester he offered a seminar under the title "On the Essence and Concept of Nature, History and the State,"[94] that is marked by Nazi thought and terminology, insisting, for instance, that a *Volk* is characterized by race and blood; perhaps it goes further in that direction than the rectoral address. But the reader can see (a) that there is nothing of this sort to be found in his writings and utterances before 1933, and (b) that such rhetoric ceases after 1934. For example, his seminar from the Winter Semester 1934–35 ("Hegel on the State")[95] is, notwithstanding Faye's insinuations, nothing more than a sober, scholarly analysis of Hegelian political philosophy.[96] The evidence is that Heidegger, a man with no political experience and little if any reading in law and political history, was caught up in a wave of euphoria at the onset of Hitler's regime and began to utter radical pro-Nazi opinions, many of them printed in bulletins of Freiburg University. But Heidegger ceased engaging in such activities after about a year.

Let us look at a few examples, drawing on his lectures and his deeds as rector. We cannot avoid noticing the political character of the **33–34** lectures on Plato. Both the courses of the rectoral year are unusually brief, and the second one is unusual also in that Heidegger did not write it out in manuscript but lectured freely, using his transcript of **31–32** (the published text of **33–34** is drawn mainly from a student transcript). There was, however, a new course Introduction and a polemical Digression, both written out by Heidegger, and both political in character. The Introduction of November 1933 brings before his hearers the necessity of *Kampf* (struggle, war). War is the Father and King of all (89f.). And this is the serious struggle of the German people, not merely a playful *agôn* among friends. In this later course, having introduced the question of untruth, Heidegger brings the political aspect of the question to prominence, which is not irrelevant to truth and untruth but materially germane to the philosophy. For truth itself only occurs in struggle and as struggle, when it takes the field in conflict with untruth (pp. 262–3). The struggle of truth with untruth is made manifest in many passages throughout the lectures, but Heidegger never wavers from the implication that the German people are to find the truth of their own being through struggle with their enemies. By contrast, it is evident that there was no political pathos or address in **31–32**, a contrast that is always elided by commentators who look for Nazism everywhere in Heidegger's works before 1933. The lecture courses of 1933 and 1934 show a *newly politicized* Heidegger with the zeal of a convert.

We should look more closely at his rhetoric in the political passages. The course opens with rhetorical salutations of a national breakthrough:

> **With the original courage of our being-here, directed forwards, we hearken back to the voices of the great inception – not so as to become Greeks and Greek-like, but rather to perceive the primordial laws of our German ethnicity in their most simple exigency and greatness.** (p. 89)

It is Heraclitus he is invoking, with his appeal to *polemos*, war:

> **[I]t does not mean *agōn*, a competition in which two friendly opponents measure their strengths, but rather the struggle of war. This means that the struggle is in earnest; the opponent is not a partner but an enemy.** (p. 90)

And this leads to further explanations that surely awaken our concern and suspicion:

> **The enemy does not have to be external, and the external enemy is not even always the most dangerous one ... The enemy can have attached itself to the innermost roots of the being-here of a people and can set itself against this people's own essence and act against it ... [We need] to cultivate and intensify a constant readiness and to prepare the attack, looking far ahead with the goal of total annihilation [*Vernichtung*].** (p. 91)

The external enemies here are surely the powers that imposed Versailles upon Germany. But who would be the internal enemies Heidegger had in mind? It seems they are found within the nation but posing a threat to it (to its essence); they can attach themselves to the innermost roots of the being of the people, and it seems the struggle is supposed to bring total annihilation to that enemy. Who can he have in mind here? Communists? Liberals? Jews?

The record of Heidegger's speeches and of his decrees as rector[97] does show at least one target that he might have had in mind: *politischer Katholizismus,* as it was called at that time. During the winter months of 1933–34 he was fighting against Catholic influence at Freiburg University. In correspondence with the Ministry of Education in Karlsruhe, 22 December and 17 February (items no. 119 and 134 in *GA 16*, pp. 224 and 250), Heidegger was aiming to fill the chair of Church History in the Faculty of Theology with a scholar whose loyalty to the German people and state would surpass any loyalty to the Church. He wanted to circumvent the nominations coming from the faculty, and also to prevent any meddling from the Roman Curia. On another occasion, 5 February 1934 (no. 131, p. 246), Heidegger wrote to the national leader of the German Students' Federation, demanding that the rights and charter of the Catholic student fraternity at Freiburg University be cancelled. A broader pattern of anti-Catholicism is manifested in Heidegger's actions during the rectorate, as has been established by Hugo Ott in the book I have already mentioned, *Martin Heidegger: A Political Life.*

This may have been on his mind during his lecture course on Plato. I believe he was telling his students there was an enemy living within the *Volk* that might also be active within the students' own minds and consciousness. We may broaden our view of the evidence once again.

This course was begun 7 November 1933, and met twice weekly, so the Heraclitus portion we quoted was probably delivered on 7 or 9 November. The editor tells us (p. 300) that this was a newly composed Introduction that Heidegger wrote by hand, and I believe it can be dated sometime between September and November 1933, after the end of the previous Summer Semester course. In October 1933, Hitler announced to the world that Germany would withdraw from the League of Nations, but to re-enforce his choice he arranged for a nationwide plebiscite on the issue, to be held on 12 November 1933. Heidegger became one of a number of leading academics to support this cause. He was photographed at a congress of German academicians meeting to support Hitler's policy on 11 November in Leipzig,[98] and he issued a statement on 10 November, where we read:

> **In this plebiscite, the *Führer* gives the people the immediate choice of the highest free decision, whether it, the whole people, wills its own existence or does not will it …**
>
> **This ultimate choice permits no hesitation or wavering – the choice reaches out to the uttermost limits of the being of our people …**
>
> **The demand is made of the people to preserve and save its own essence … A clear will to self-responsibility for enduring the destiny of our people has required of the *Führer* to withdraw from the League of Nations.**[99]

While campaigning for the plebiscite, then, Heidegger has identified an internal enemy that could bring weakness or confusion, an inadequate or divided loyalty. And I read the Introduction to the Plato lectures in a similar way. Heidegger is telling his students that they should not betray Germany because of other commitments. They have the bold choice to follow the *Führer* and to defy the world, and anyone who shrinks from that is yielding to the enemy within. Of course, he may have intended yet further enemies besides the Church.

We now have further documents of Heidegger's thinking from the 1930s that were not available to his many critics between 1945 and 2010: Division IV of *GA*, comprising volumes 89–102; most of these volumes are not yet published, but we do have volumes 94 to 96, published in 2014, incorporating fourteen of Heidegger's "Black Notebooks," notes composed between 1931 and 1941. The editor, Peter Trawny, recognizes[100] that they resemble other thinkers' diaries, and that is how I too have read them: notations arranged chronologically and not thematically, sometimes referring to events of the day, sometimes drafting philosophical ideas. We find observations about Heidegger's social environment, often coloured by his personal feelings, expressed in a more direct style than in the *Contributions*.

GA 94 contains entries that Heidegger made during the period of his rectorate at Freiburg University and in the immediate aftermath of it (pp. 103–99). After that, the volume offers many sour remarks about

Germany in the 1930s: the *völkisch* culture, the confused younger generation, the mediocre intellectuals. One notable emphasis is the disdain he exhibits towards churches both Catholic and Protestant. The central fault of modern Christianity is that is has declined into a "cultural style," identifying itself so thoroughly with modernity that it has nothing left to proclaim (*GA* 95, pp. 4–5, 110–11, 284). He particularly excoriates the Protestant *Deutsche Christen* as simply a neo-pagan cult serving Nazism (*GA* 94, p. 522). But he has no time either for the other Protestant current, the Confessing Church with its theologian Karl Barth (*GA* 95, pp. 395–6) or for the papal concordat with Germany's regime (*GA* 95, p. 5).

But what is most incendiary in this publication is that Heidegger also speaks reproachfully here about Jews and Judaism. In the first place, he sees the Jews as committing the exact opposite fault from the Christians: they are so utterly detached from the "world" that they tend to undermine all culture (see vol. 96, pp. 46–7). Further comments on Jews and "world Judaism" (*Weltjudentum*) led to a scandal when they were finally published in 2014. The *GA*'s editor himself, Peter Trawny, published a critique[101] that saw anti-Semitism raised here to a new level, embellished with the history of being. And indeed, there are entries that attribute unpleasant characteristics to Jews in volume 96, pages 46–7 and 56–7. Trawny cited these two extracts on pages 18–19 of his book (English translation). In the first, probably dating from 1939, Heidegger attributes an empty rationality and calculative skill to the Jewish people. In the second, probably also from 1939, Heidegger stresses an exaggerated Jewish attachment to their own race. Then, as a third extract, Trawny cites *GA* 96, page 133, which is of a later date, probably 1941, where Heidegger is concerned about an international Jewish conspiracy against Germany. These anti-Semitic remarks are a stain on Heidegger's legacy and have led some readers to reject the man and the philosophy as anti-Semitic. But I believe Trawny's approach is flawed.

He says (pp. 20–37) that the remarks we have cited were expressed in the terminology of Heidegger's "history of being," *Seinsgeschichte.* That is debatable, but even if true it would not show that the *Seinsgeschichte* itself had an anti-Semitic motivation, though that is the case Trawny is making. The remarks we've cited date from 1939–41, years in which Hitler's war against the West was looming or had already begun. I believe the remarks are politically driven, not philosophically driven – that they express Heidegger's fears about the immediate future of Germany in a time of crisis. But Heidegger had begun work on the *Seinsgeschichte* in 1930 or 1931 (we shall have more to say about it in Part II). There are no remarks whatever about the Jews in those years or the intervening years. Trawny overplays his hand most egregiously on pages 92–4.

Moreover, we now have further newly published correspondence between Heidegger and his brother Fritz, from the years of the First World War until after the Second World War[102] – a singular text indeed, for this book contains essays from several critics excoriating Heidegger's "anti-Semitism," accompanied by extracts from his correspondence to document the charge – except that the correspondence contains not the slightest hint of anti-Semitism!

It is no easy matter to decide what use should be made, in philosophical critiques, of private diaries and correspondence among family members. For my part, I recognize them as evidence for the thoughts, opinions, and attitudes of Heidegger, but for the critic and scholar they cannot have the same weight as published books and articles, or well-documented deeds. To be weighed against the accumulated evidence that Heidegger's critics have brought, I believe that history affords two essential facts:

(1) that not one of Heidegger's students ever became implicated in National Socialism or its crimes, despite postwar allegations that Heidegger was a bad influence, a corrupter of youth;
(2) that Heidegger never took practical measures to harm any Jew.

I have been referring to "political storms" of 1933 that buffeted Heidegger, but his entire life thereafter and his legacy of writings have been engulfed in political storms begotten by 1933; they have not subsided; if anything, they have gained in intensity up to today. Is Heidegger's work of thinking – the sort that we are reviewing in this book – compromised by his political adventure or by the evidence we have of his thoughts and prejudices? The critics who have said so are usually motivated to find some element in his work that must be rejected: Heidegger on truth, or on being, or on history, or the whole thing. But "the Heidegger Case"[103] is not one of simple opposition between pro- and anti-phenomenology, or pro- and anti-Nazism, or even pro- and anti-Heidegger. I would suggest instead that Heidegger's life and work exhibited a cleft or bifurcation that many of his readers, especially his critics, have not noticed, have not understood, and consequently have misunderstood grievously. They think of the rector in Freiburg, of the influential professor, and of course of the 102 volumes of his *Collected Works*, and the great weight of this academic success thrown into the balance of Germany's political divisions, as helping to bring a temporary triumph to the Nazis. Of course, the critics are also aware that the man himself emerged from an obscure background, not in Freiburg but in the town of Messkirch in the Upper Danube, with its rural, provincial culture quite backward compared to

Freiburg with its university and bishopric, bordering on Switzerland and France. So they allege that it was an antimodern peasantry that guided Heidegger into right-wing politics and then finally into its most virulent form. Such was the reading proposed by Victor Farias about three decades ago, and though much commentary has come since then, I think his appraisal of Heidegger speaks for many critics to this day.[104] I offered a reply to that reading,[105] on which I'd like to draw now. We should not link the rural, conservative, peasant-oriented culture of Messkirch on the Upper Danube to Heidegger's option for National Socialism. The latter was a national movement, driven by factions in Munich, Berlin, and other big urban centres; it was a current of modernity, and the student movement that influenced Heidegger in Freiburg was a national one. Heidegger as rector was caught up in frantic movement, constantly on the move, forming alliances with rectors at other German universities, sending telegrams to Karlsruhe and Berlin.

Behind his frantic activities during this time, there was his memory of his ancestral *Heimat*, its meadows, brooks, country lanes, old barns and houses, workshops, its St Martin's Church – and its dialect. Heidegger delighted in both writing and speaking this dialect; he was deeply attached to the Allemanian poet Johann Peter Hebel, a sort of South German Robert Burns, and wrote many essays about him, in some of them trying out the dialect himself.[106] In March 1934, just at the time he was preparing to resign as rector, he gave the bucolic radio address "Why Stay in the Province?," which expressed his lifelong attachment to his southern *Heimat* as the reason for refusing calls to Berlin University. A later expression of this provincialism was his pronounced preference for the French region of Provence over Paris.

Specific to Heidegger's personality was his ability to combine the rational atmosphere of the big university, and philosophy, with the age-old know-how of the peasant, the *bricoleur*, who can speak in dialect. This made him a figure very difficult for many observers to understand. He was a small, obscure man of the provinces, yet he came to enjoy a remarkable fame. He was a peasant, yet he wore the robes of the Freiburg rector, *Seine Magnifizenz*. He had attended only one university, yet he could cut up Cassirer, Rickert, and Jaspers. This was for many who observed him a riddle, and it awakened suspicion, dislike, and contempt among some of his contemporaries – by no means all! – and it has continued to affect some of his readers – certainly not all! – up to today. Critics found it difficult to articulate this dislike, so it often expressed itself in the form of a political critique: "He is/was a Nazi!" – which was easy to articulate.

PART II

Later Work

The Pathway Rectified

In the earlier chapters of *WW* 1949, I see a continued adherence to phenomenology, but in a rectified form: the 1930 version brought out clearly the central role of conduct, and therefore freedom, in the constitution of truth, but it did not have a sure command of other factors, cooperating with free conduct, that are required to constitute truth: the Over-against that accounts for the status of Object that the thing attains; the Open as the element in which the Over-against is possible; the character of the thing as "that which is present," which is to be interpreted also as "that which is (*das Seiende*)." For these reasons, the 1949 account is less subjectively coloured.

Units 2 to 5 here show what new elaboration was required for the phenomenology of the statement and experience; then the following Unit 6 shows how the later version strengthened the connection of this phenomenology to the ancient experience of *alētheia.*

After 1930, or rather 1934, Heidegger moved to correct the overconfident doctrine of his earlier period that an a priori *Seinsverständnis* gave guidance to the sciences in their grasp of beings. We shall see below that, in 1943 and 1949, the experience of truth is not specifically accomplished by the sciences but can be traced in every human encounter with the world. In these encounters, there is an unveiling, not only of the *object* in its Over-against, not only of the *thing* in the Open, but of *beings, das Seiende,* that take on the status of what is present, *das Anwesende* (see below, end of Unit 4 and end of Unit 5).

These developments have a counterpart in Heidegger's awareness of the political world. After 1934, he began to move away from the National Socialism that had bewitched his judgment in 1933 – a gradual emancipation, by all the available evidence. Someone who has been strongly and sincerely held by a political doctrine of that sort will not usually perform a sudden *volte face,* a 180-degree reversal like St Paul's conversion on the road to Damascus. Rather, there is a slow withdrawal of the earlier convictions. Heidegger did not begin to say what some of his critics seem to demand of him: "Now I see that American democracy is better than National Socialism." Rather, there are small separate indications of a change in this view or that one. In his Freiburg lectures on Hölderlin in 1934–35,[107] he is explicit is repudiating the view that the German *Volk* can be understood as a biological type owing to their blood and soil – rather, the people are constituted by their history and language, and it is their poets who are the guides to the people. We can also see, later in the 1930s, how he repudiates the *Führerprinzip* that left such a mark on his rectoral address. In notes that can be dated sometime after 1936,[108] he speaks scornfully of self-styled "*Führers*" who are nothing more in fact than administrative workers in the modern system of technology, in which peace is simply the continuation of war by other means and the world contains nothing more than raw materials for consumption. Such notes as these confirm Heidegger's assertion in the *Spiegel* interview that, in his courses in the 1930s, he had communicated a continuing criticism of National Socialism.

Throughout Part II, we treat some of the history in which *alētheia* and other variants of truth show their interaction, injecting new complexity into the essence of truth. Thus, in the 1949 version we are able to trace more completely the role of history (*Geschichte*) as fate (*Geschick*), where the original experience of truth undergoes alterations over time.

The essence of truth has receded into the past – yet it remains effective nevertheless![109] We want to see the disguises and mutations of *alētheia*, tracing it from the Greeks up to modern philosophy. We look beneath the mask, beneath the skin, of alternative accounts of truth. We call this "fate" (*Geschick*), recognizing in that term the essence of history (*Geschichte*). Part of Heidegger's diagnosis is offered in his account of Plato and how his thought departed from the primordial experience, and Part II, A, opens with that. Our study will incorporate chapters from the history in which *alētheia* underwent its mutations, beginning with Plato's treatment of truth, which shows both unconcealedness and correctness.

Then Part II will comment on the 1949 version of *WW*, with a few explicit contrasts with the 1930 version. This longer scrutiny of *WW* 1949 runs from its chapter 1 through its chapter 4, and the key movement takes us from correctness back to the earliest institution of truth, where unconcealedness was established by the Presocratic thinkers; thus the phenomenology will be running backwards, as it were, through the history, going from correctness to the deeper underlying unconcealedness. With this attention to the *Seinsgeschichte*, the exposition in Part II will not follow literally the course of the pathway, as Part I did, even though, as

I stated in introducing Part I, the arcs of the pathway do appear clearly in the 1949 text. Treatment of the pathway will be interrupted by some chapters of the history of truth. Part II, B, will introduce a chapter from the Medieval Scholastics (as Heidegger does explicitly in 1949), in which divine governance is established as the precondition for truth. Our account then turns to chapter 5 of *WW* and some later phases of the history, especially of the Rationalists of modernity. Then in Part II, C, we see how our technological civilization has come completely to obscure the primordial *alētheia*, the phenomenon of untruth covering over the primordial experience.

Finally, the last units of Part II will confront the hardest questions: whether there was an inadequacy in the entire early pathway of thinking, not only in its treatment of truth but altogether – whether the thinking of being had misconstrued the status of beings, whether the thinking had overplayed itself, whether concealment would need to conquer it in the end. The ancient Greeks had an original experience (*Erfahrung*) of unconcealedness – they achieved this at the moment when they posed the most primordial of all questions, "What is *das Seiende, ti to on*?" Though we are removed from their experience, it is a central implication of Heidegger's view of *essence* that such circumstances do not obliterate the primordial granting of truth as *alētheia*; the essence retains its authority even through the history that suppressed it.

(A) Unconcealedness and Correctness

1. The Plato Lectures

A significant point is added to Heidegger's account of truth in chapter 1 of the published versions of 1943 and 1949, at the end of **1.4**. We read that the concept of truth as accordance conceives truth as correctness or rightness. It is explained that every accordance

> **has continually in view a conforming to – [*sich richten nach* –] and hence thinks truth as correctness [*Richtigkeit*].**

This reference to correctness does help the contemporary reader assimilate Heidegger's account. If we take the adequation of statement and thing as the usual *definition* of truth, we can say that it *implies* the *equation* of truth with correctness. The many virtual synonyms for correct – right, accurate, faithful – are commonly understood to capture the nature of truth in scientific work, legal settings, journalistic inquiry, and so on.

The equation of truth with correctness plays a role in **1.4**: the *Richtigkeit* of the statement is conditioned by the *Richtmass* (standard, gauge) that the conduct has allowed the thing to set for it. Here the double idea – the self-opening conduct, and the thing's standard – finds expression. It is the openness of our conduct that is the ground and prototype of the truth of the statement. And here the point is stated, more clearly than in 1930, that truth is not confined to the statement. In **2.4**:

> **A statement is invested with its correctness by the openness of conduct ... If the correctness (truth) of statements becomes possible only through the openness of conduct, then what first makes correctness possible must with more original legitimacy be taken as the essence of truth.**

Moreover, **2.3** had concluded:

> **Speech that directs itself accordingly [speaking of beings such-as they are] is correct (true). What is thus said is the correct (the true).**

And in chapter 3, we find the prominent italicized declaration:

> ***The essence of truth, as the correctness of a statement, is freedom.***

This identification goes hand in hand with what Heidegger has called the "usual concept of truth" in chapter 1.

Yet it is a significant fact that in the original 1930 text of the address *WW there was not a single reference to correctness.* The barest reference to the *adaequatio* doctrine in Section I(a) made no reference to correctness at all. So it was only in revising *WW* for publication that Heidegger changed the wording, introducing "correct." Moreover, *there was no reference to correctness in the text of SZ.* And I believe one could scrutinize Heidegger's phenomenological works of the 1920s without finding any reference to correctness, or any suggestion that truth should be interpreted as correctness. This presents a puzzle, and it would seem to be an important issue because there are many other occasions when Heidegger sets out a major *opposition* between conceiving truth as unconcealedness and conceiving it as correctness. Later chapters of *WW* seem to assume a direct confrontation between truth *qua* unconcealedness and the variant of truth that he calls "correctness" – for example, this sentence from **4.7**:

> **"Truth" is not a feature of correct propositions that are asserted of an "object" by a human "subject" and then "are valid" somewhere, in what sphere we know not; rather truth is disclosure of beings through which an openness essentially unfolds.**

Heidegger's use of scare quotes indicates that here he is targeting a common conception current in his age, that includes several aspects: the common conception assigns truth to statements or propositions as a feature of them; this truth can be identified as their correctness, *Richtigkeit*; such a statement is produced by a "subject" and refers to an "object"; truth itself is "being-valid," *Gelten.*

These points were certainly of broad provenance and can be found in many sources in modern philosophy. But here, in **4.7**, Heidegger is roundly denying them all. This is striking because at earlier stages of the essay he had implicitly been identifying truth with correctness. How could a pathway accomplish a turning such as this: proceeding from the study of a statement that is true in the sense of correct, to a situation where we discover a truth that stands opposed to correctness and to the other features that accompany this correctness? Heidegger himself guides us towards that reflection when he tells us, in **4.3** that to translate *alētheia* as "unconcealedness" rather than as "truth" "**contains the directive to rethink the ordinary concept of truth in the sense of the correctness of statements and to think it back to**" disclosedness and deconcealment of beings.

I shall be making the case that this relationship is *not* a conceptual one or an analytic one, but is essentially a historical issue, an issue of *Geschick* or fate.

The Parable of the Cave

The relationship between unconcealedness and correctness first entered Heidegger's work in the course of lectures he devoted to Plato in the 1930s: (a) the lectures of 1931–32: *On the Essence of Truth: On Plato's Cave Allegory and "Theaetetus"*; and (b) lectures of 1933–34: *On the Essence of Truth.* At the very start of **31–32**, page 2, Heidegger introduces the point that truth has come to be identified as correctness, *Richtigkeit.* On pages 11–12, Heidegger sees this just as *our own customary prejudice,* in contrast with the ancient *alētheia.* Our modern correctness attaches to statements, whereas *alētheia* was ascribed to things. But then a decisive step in this lecture's Introduction is taken, on page 17, when Heidegger adds the claim that there was in ancient times a transition, *Übergang,* from Unconcealment to Correctness: "**Western philosophy takes off on an erroneous and fateful course**" (p. 17). And in **33–34**, we find a sharp contrast:

> ***A-lētheia,* unconcealment, is taken from the factual situation of concealing, veiling, or in turn unveiling and unconcealing. "Correctness" is taken from the factual situation of the directedness of something towards something, from the factual situation of gauging and measuring. "Unveiling" and "measuring" are entirely different factual situations.** (p. 98)

We must ask: could these two have any inner connection? (p. 98). In **33–34** we find further descriptions of each of these distinct versions (pp. 121, 165).

We'll focus first on the **31–32** course. Part I of this course is intended to elicit the many variations of *alētheia* in the Cave allegory of the *Republic*: one manifestation of it in the original position below in the cave; another at the point where the prisoner begins his escape; another at the point where the prisoner exits from the cave; all of this under Heidegger's title "The Clue to the 'Essence' of *Alētheia.*" Offered less than a year after the December 1930 address, the course has many echoes of it. Heidegger begins by probing the problematic relationship between statement and thing, analysing their correspondence, *Übereinstimmung* (pp. 2–3); here too he contrasts this case with that of true gold (pp. 3–4); and he leads the discussion back to *alētheia* (pp. 10–19). Above all, the course follows the same overall architecture as the address in that it leads up to a strong positive bond between truth and untruth; that is accomplished in Part II of the course through an interpretation of the *Theaetetus* that will concern us below. Heidegger offered *Vom Wesen der Wahrheit* again as a course in **33–34**, though it was considerably shortened. There is a great deal here too that recalls the 1930 address. Like the opening of the address, it begins by questioning whether we need to ask about the essence of truth, by contrast with the real, practical "truths" that correspond to human needs (pp. 83–5); again it argues that no practical urgency can bypass the question of essence. He continues to analyse *Übereinstimmung*, even using the same example, "The coin is round" (pp. 121–3). Again, Part One is devoted to the Cave allegory: what it says about *alētheia*; and Part II treats untruth by way of the *Theaetetus*.

The main point of Heidegger, while recognizing that *alētheia* remains at work in Plato, is that in the Cave allegory Plato is moving to conceive truth as correctness. We can see the main points in Heidegger's comment on Socrates's retrospective interpretation, *Rep.* 517 a 8–518 d 8. In my exposition, I'll cite the later text *PLW*[110] because it allows us to consult in economical form all the texts of the Cave allegory (515 c 2, d 6–7, 516 a 3, and, in Socrates's retrospective interpretation, 517 c 4) that use the word *alētheia* in one form or another, while Heidegger's lecture-commentaries treated them more exhaustively. One motive for Heidegger's interpretation is that, interwoven with those texts, there are a few (515 a 4, 517 c 2) that substitute the word *orthotēs*, "correctness," for *alētheia*.

But now we must examine more carefully the confrontation between truth *qua* correctness and truth *qua* unconcealedness.

First, a clarification. The Greeks did have a "natural concept of truth." We find it in Homer and other authors, where a speaker calls someone's words *alēthes*, and in this everyday context it means true *qua* correct (*richtig*) or reliable (*verlässlich*), two senses of truth that cannot be equated with unconcealedness. There was no etymological resonance in this use of the word among the Greeks. This is a point Heidegger later acknowledges in "The End of Philosophy and the Task of Thinking."[111] His thesis of *Seinsgeschichte* is not abandoned, however, for it deals, not with ordinary parlance, but with the subtle interactions with the texts of philosophy, especially Parmenides. He is recognizing a pragmatic, non-etymological use of *alēthes*, one that is older than Parmenides and that stands in contrast to his goddess's monumental invocation of unconcealedness. The argument that *Alētheia* means unconcealedness has its application *only* to Parmenides and other thinkers, not to the Greek language as a whole. The main point that emerges from the history is that a thinker *can* give a monumental force to a word like *Alētheia* that otherwise circulates in discourse in another, everyday sense. Heidegger pointed out often[112] that this was also the case with Plato's word *idea*. We need to recognize from the start that Heidegger's analysis is not based only, or mainly, on the occurrence of the word *orthotēs*, or on the etymology of *alētheia*, but on Plato's philosophical points as well.

We should note one detail of *PLW*. Heidegger had often drawn upon archaic Greek expressions, and some Presocratic texts, in establishing his interpretation of *alētheia* as unconcealedness. But it is notable that in *PLW*, he takes care to offer evidence that Plato's own thought *was* marked by an original understanding of *alētheia* in this sense. For Heidegger, the archaic view of *alētheia* was presupposed by Plato when he conceived and wrote the allegory of the Cave:

> **This "allegory" can have the structure of a cave image at all only because it is antecedently co-determined by the fundamental experience of *alētheia*, the unhiddenness of beings, which was something self-evident for the Greeks. For what else is the underground cave except something open in itself that remains at the same time covered by a vault and, despite the entrance, walled off and enclosed by the surrounding earth? This cave-like enclosure that is open within itself, and that which surrounds it and therefore hides, both refer at the same time to an outside, the unhidden that is spread out in the light above ground. Only the essence of truth understood in the original Greek sense of *alētheia* – the unhiddenness that is related to the hidden (to something dissembled and disguised) – has an essential relation to this image of an underground cave. Wherever truth has another essence, wherever it is not unhiddenness or at least is not co-determined by unhiddenness, there an "allegory of the cave" has no basis as an illustration.**[113]

This is an important recognition of *alētheia* in Plato.

The Ideas and the Good

Throughout his commentary, Heidegger has been expressing his reading of the ideas – including the idea of the Good – as crucially informed by seeing and by light:

> **Every idea, the visible form of something, provides a look at what a being is in each case. Thus in Greek thinking the "ideas" enable something to appear in its whatness and thus be present in its constancy**[114] **... The ideas are what is in everything that is.**[115]

And this feature of the Idea is no less applicable to the idea of the Good:

> **As idea the good is something that shines, thus something that produces vision, thus in turn something visible and hence knowable.**[116]

Here he quotes Socrates at 517 b 8:

> **In the sphere of what can be known, the idea of the good is the power of visibility that accomplishes all shining forth and that therefore is properly seen only last, in fact it is hardly (only with great pains) really seen at all.**

The Good is of course also an idea, and has along with the others the relation to vision and light: the idea of the Good is infused with intelligibility and light. But it is also special: Heidegger stress its character as *tauglich-machen* – the good is that which makes fit and able:

> **What makes every idea be capable as an idea – in Plato's expression the idea of all ideas – consists in making possible the appearing, in all its visibility, of everything present ... Therefore the idea of ideas is that-which-enables as such, *to agathon* – "The good" grants the appearing of the visible form in which whatever is present has its stability in that which it is.**[117]

Heidegger, in all his lectures and essays, calls attention to the manner in which light, and the Good as the source of the light, bring together the eye and the visible thing, and supernally, link together our *nous* and the intelligible things. This is accomplished in the first instance by *alētheia*. But now he says, drawing on Socrates's interpretation, that in 517–18 Socrates brings *alētheia* under the yoke of the idea of the good. This is the mainspring of Heidegger's interpretation – its basis is the line [Grube translation]:

> **[The idea of the good], when seen, must be reckoned to be for all the cause of all that is right and beautiful, to have produced in the visible world both light and the fount of light, while in the intelligible world it is itself that which produces and controls truth and intelligence.** (517 c)

The importance of this is that now the *nous* must direct itself to the idea, and that will be the whole tendency of Platonic philosophy from this point on; and indeed of later philosophy – Heidegger mentions the medievals and modern science. Truth is ascribed to the intellect when it has measured itself against the idea. Therefore truth has become correctness, the content of *nous* measured against the idea. This intellectualism, as I'd call it, is the progenitor of metaphysics and science. This mutation appears not only in Socrates's interpretation of the Cave allegory – it also is visible in later works of Plato, notably *Sophist* 263 a-b. Here the Eleatic Visitor undertakes to differentiate a true statement (*alēthes logos*) from a false one (*pseudes*). What the former says of a thing is just how the thing is, while the latter says of it something other than what is. And we see many traces of this in later tradition, beginning in Aristotle, whose *Metaphysics (Gamma,* 7) offered essentially the same account: "To say of what is that it is not, or of what is not that it is, is false, while to say of what is that it is, and of what is not that it is not, is true" (1011 b 26–7).

Criticisms and Replies

The Plato readings have attracted much unfavourable attention over the years, with Plato scholars leading the attack.[118] We look especially at Gonzalez. His appraisal of *PLW* is harsh, and his footnotes to those pages cite judgments of many other scholars in agreement with him.[119] Heidegger's readings of the text are characterized as erroneous (p. 151) and dishonest (p. 150), owing to his insistence on seeing Plato's system ("Platonism") as an event in the history of metaphysics. The present study cannot undertake a complete review of the criticisms from Gonzalez and others, and we must leave open the question whether Heidegger's texts succeed as interpretations of Plato's texts.

Gonzalez and other critics want to defend Plato from the historical thesis of Heidegger's *Seinsgeschichte*; they want to promote what they see as a natural, open-minded reading of Plato's text, to receive instruction from Plato. Surely this is an interest we can all recognize and endorse. But does it follow that Plato *cannot* be read historically, as one document in the history of metaphysics, or, for that matter, as one document in the history of Greek politics, or literature, or religion? Surely not! A close reading of Plato, open to being instructed by him, is ideally our first reading of the text, but it should not be invoked in order to prevent a second reading that treats the text historically as a document in succession to other documents, and followed by yet others, as evidence of the history of metaphysics (politics, literary style, religion). Besides that general issue, there are several specific objections we find in Gonzalez.

What gives special offence to Plato scholars here, I believe, is the claim of the radically split and dichotomous constitution of truth that Plato bequeathed to Western metaphysics. Gonzalez differs from many of Heidegger's critics in that he not only accepts the idea that unconcealedness was the prime meaning of truth in ancient Greece, but also wants to document the persistent, uncontaminated working of unconcealedness in the thought of Plato, which he had inherited from the Greek language and from the earliest thinkers. He disputes Heidegger's view that the character of Platonic philosophy was defined by the transition in which *alētheia* was replaced by *orthotēs.*

Gonzalez also objects to the intimate connection Heidegger has posited between the idea, on the one hand, and light and seeing, on the other. On pages 120–1, Gonzalez comments on **31–32**, where Heidegger identifies the idea with light, but he objects, in that "while the idea might provide the light within which a particular sensible object appears as what it is, the idea cannot provide the light without *itself being illuminated.*" And later (p. 153), commenting on *PLW*, Gonzalez objects to rendering the term "idea" as "the look" of something, for that subordinates it to the event of seeing. But these points overlook the phenomenological character of Heidegger's reading, in which the idea is interpreted in terms of the experiences in which it has become manifest. Gonzalez, instead, is correcting such details with the aid of a literal reading of Plato's metaphysical conclusions about the Sun and its light. Of course he cannot deny the essential experiential connection of Ideas to seeing and to light. Heidegger's treatment of the Ideas showed that when we encounter something, it is the Idea that lets us see *what* it is and that conveys its being to our apprehension. Yet oddly, Gonzalez is also exasperated by Heidegger's *minimizing* the role of light in the simile of the Sun (Gonzalez, pp. 122–36), which is undoubtedly a heritage of Parmenides and the primordial analogy between light and unconcealedness.

Gonzalez also objects to Heidegger's interpretation of the yoke. He thinks Heidegger has uprooted this metaphor from its place in the analogy of the Sun and applied it unduly to the Cave allegory. Where Plato had posited light as the yoke that united eye and the visible, and supernally united *nous* with the intelligible, he accuses Heidegger of mistaking the metaphor, and setting up the sun itself as a yoke that links *nous* together with truth, *alētheia* (pp. 122–4). But this does *not* appear in the **31–32** exposition! And the schema that Gonzalez ascribes to Heidegger at the top of page 136 is quite at odds with the schemas Heidegger himself used for the analogy of the Sun (**31–32**, pp. 106, 326).[120]

What Is Seinsgeschichte*?*

If we consult *Contributions to Philosophy*, 1936–38, nos. 209–11, 230–3, as well as *Plato's Doctrine of Truth*, 1942 (*PLW*), we see a trajectory in the Plato interpretations, expressing the intrusion of *orthotēs, correctness,* at the expense of *alētheia*, a tendency to drive correctness and unconcealedness farther and farther apart, combined with the historical narrative.

Lying in this study, however, is a point that seems to me most important, and that is often lost sight of in the commentaries on Heidegger: the two concepts of truth, unconcealedness and correctness, have an inner connection, they are intertwined with each other, as Heidegger asserted in the very earliest of his Plato lectures, **31–32**. ***[E]ine Verstrickung … ineinander gewirrt sind*** (p. 17). In the latest of the studies, "Plato's Doctrine of Truth," he refers to the double character of truth as an ambiguity.[121] It is the task of *Seinsgeschichte* to bring to light the multifarious constitution of truth, both in Plato himself and in the development of metaphysics throughout the centuries. We read on the same page that this ambiguity was transmitted to Plato's successors, for Aristotle's *Metaphysics* has just this double sense of truth, correctness in Gamma 7 but undoubtedly unconcealedness in Theta 10.

This is how we are to understand Heidegger's *Seinsgeschichte.* When our comprehension of this matter is truly historical, in the relevant sense, it overcomes the sharpness of opposition that Heidegger's critics took such exception to, one conception of truth brutally shoved aside in favour of another. When we grasp that Plato, Aristotle, and the later tradition too are shaped by an ambiguous co-presence of both forms of truth, we see that it is not the displacement of one by the other, but rather a process of mutation that still preserves some force of the original – what we should rather understand as the *metamorphosis* of unconcealedness into correctness. In a metamorphosis the original subject is still in some way saved. Unconcealedness has not been consigned to the dustbin of history, but remains with us still, still a part of the constitution of truth, along with correctness. Unconcealedness has not been extinguished in this *Geschichte* – rather, it has retreated behind its successor, correctness. But its continuing force can be noted even in the inquiry we are studying here, Heidegger's *WW*, especially the 1949 version. As the phenomenological study of truth *qua* correctness in chapter 2 proceeds to its conclusion, it is able to look behind the Over-against in which statement and object confront each other, to reveal the Open, into which the thing makes its entrance and the speaker makes his or her entrance. As the meditation continues, it identifies this Open as the freedom that was the essence of truth in chapter 3. Then in chapter 4, this freedom reveals its own essence as the kind of dwelling in the Open that Heidegger calls letting-be, and here unconcealedness shows itself. All these structures can now be recognized as the traces of unconcealedness that persevere within correctness. Therefore, despite the innovations of Plato and metaphysics, unconcealedness remains the *essence* of truth, still authoritative even if withdrawn into hiding. Moreover, the further development of our main text *WW* confirms this: in the chapters that follow, we see that even as truth (unconcealedness) is submerged in concealment and in error, its inner constitution remains that of *alētheia.* Such is the force of an inquiry into the *essence* of truth. At the end of Part II, I shall make the case that truth in science – modern science, that is – manifests the very dual character I find in Plato.

Every inquiry that Heidegger institutes into the essence of truth also brings into the foreground the factor of untruth. It cannot be a mere afterthought, something left over after the main business is done. It is part of the main business. After studying the allegory of the Cave to highlight the twofold constitution of truth that Plato bequeathed to Western metaphysics, both lecture courses conclude the exposition with the return of the philosopher to the kingdom of shadows, and this occasions the shift of topic to a discussion of Untruth. Our question is how these two cohere: why the intimate tie to the essence of truth? In the first place, the connection is existential, because the essence of truth (and of untruth) is directly linked with our own historical essence as human beings (**33–34**, 178). It is an urgent and existential calling of the philosopher to confront the untruth that he alone is in a position to recognize: those shadows in the cave that do have their own mode of Unconcealedness, even though ultimately they constitute a Concealment. His mission is to pull others out of their chains:

> **With the return of the liberated prisoner into the cave, he realizes above all that in unison with unconcealment, concealment, semblance and deception happen and must happen ... unconcealment happens in history, in the constant confrontation with the false and with semblance.** (**33–34**, 184)
>
> **... Untruth is not simply truth's opposite; rather, only as confrontation is truth as unconcealment cast into untruth and embedded there.** (**33–34**, 187)

Part II will devote more discussion to untruth in Section (C) below. Now we return to *WW* 1943–49.

2. The Phenomenology of 1949: Experience in *WW* 2

The following Units 2 to 6 treat chapters 2 to 4 of *WW* 1949 – we begin from an analysis of truth *qua* correctness, revealing several of its conditions; but this study will lead our thought once again to the underlying essence, unconcealedness.

The First Arc in the 1930 version led to freedom, then the Second Arc established unconcealedness as the ultimate condition for freedom. But the earlier paragraphs in Section I(b), pages 385–6, were subjected to a major rewriting in the published texts. In 1943 and 1949, in **2.2**, Heidegger drops the verb *meinen*, replacing it with the hyphenated *Vor-stellen*, signifying both "present" and "set before." This later version contains a very complex and original account of experience, one that establishes conditions for experience, for objects, for their encounter, going well beyond the treatment of 1930, which was especially focused on our intending and our conduct.

> **There is one kind of relationship that holds between a statement and a thing, and it is on the basis of that kind of relationship that this particular adequation will be determined in its essence. As long as that "relationship" itself is left undefined, and we do not see where its own essence finds its grounding, all disputing about this adequation, about its possibility or impossibility, about its character and degree, will lead nowhere. But**

> **the statement about the coin puts "itself" into relation to this thing by presenting it; it highlights a certain aspect of what is presented and it says that this thing is marked in just that way. In undertaking to present a thing, a statement will be asserting that the thing that it is presenting *is* such as the statement says. The presenting and the presented are combined in the "such-as."**[122]

We'll identify a number of distinct factors enumerated in **2.2** and **2.3** that make accordance possible, and this one, *Vor-stellen*, is the first.

Presenting

The hyphen in Heidegger's word is designed to point the reader away from the usual cognitive connotations of *Vorstellung*, commonly understood as the mental act of representing. Von Herrmann's commentary[123] stresses strongly the intentional sense of our orientation – to the thing itself and not to any mental representations. We do justice to Heidegger's intent if we imagine instead a teacher "presenting" a speaker to her class, *introducing* a speaker: "Captain Novus here was the one who rescued six injured sailors ..." The statement relates itself to the coin by presenting it and saying what it is like, according to some particular guiding perspective. Thus, in our example, the statement presents the coin with reference to its shape: the five-mark coin is round; it's not a polygon like the English pound piece. This is first of all a reference to the subject-and-predicate character of the statement, but it also introduces a second relation, the specific relation that a statement has to a thing, which Heidegger usually calls showing, or indicating, or *apophansis*:

> **What is stated by the presentative statement is said of the presented thing in just *such* manner *as* that thing, as presented, is.**

Heidegger says that the "such-as" has to do with the presenting and what it presents. What that means is that this factor, the "such-as," is *spread out* between those two: given the presented coin *as* round, the presentation expresses its *such*, something that coincides. The "*such-as*" lies in their between, that is, in their apophantic relationship. Heidegger wants now to delve into this. The predication and the apophansis form a criss-cross of two relations contained in this "such-as." Heidegger wants now to delve into this relationship of statement and thing, and he prepares the way by calling attention to two kinds of presupposition that we must consciously set aside.

(a) We cannot understand the relationship through psychology. The present essay is responding at many points to ongoing discussions about truth that had lasted several decades in Germany. The philosophical movement called psychologism was the subject of Heidegger's doctoral dissertation of 1914, *The Theory of Judgments in Psychologism.*[124] This movement tried to reduce logical principles to psychological laws, as manifestations of how the mind behaved: such an empiricist treatment of logic had to include a merely psychological treatment of truth. We see in the fourth section of the thesis that Theodor Lipps had argued that when our thinking is "objective," it is being constrained by objects, so that the mind, experiencing this as a foreign force, develops a "truth-consciousness." This is a merely subjective account of truth, and cannot be adopted here.

(b) Neither can we be guided in this by any "theory of consciousness." All during his education, Heidegger was well aware of the clash of Germany's two dominant schools, empiricist psychologism and the neo-Kantianism that tended to regard truth as an a priori "value" – the view of Heinrich Rickert. Heidegger undertook a sharp criticism of Rickert's main book, *The Object of Knowledge,* in his 1925 lectures on *Logic.* Rickert thought that in forming a judgment we postulate truth as a "value," indeed, as an eternal value. Probably Heidegger had Husserl in mind as well in this critical comment, for Husserl's theory of consciousness was that the activity of *noesis* was the agent in "constituting" the object of knowledge, what he called the *noema.*[125]

Letting the Thing Stand (Entgegenstehenlassen)

If we set those theories aside, and reach down into the sub-structure of experience that undergirds the theories, we shall be able to understand the relationship quite differently – and here is Heidegger's new and unique thrust. The purpose of our investigation is to uncover how a statement is actually possible. This will be a piece of phenomenology (though Heidegger does not use that word here), for we can see that he is engaging in a description of experience, not a mere analysis of concepts. Heidegger offers an account of experience that is entirely original and not to be found in any other text.

He begins by proposing a literal rendering of the term *Vor-stellen,* and his bracketing out theories of psychology or epistemology implies that he is proposing something so basic that it underlies all such theories:

> ***Vor-stellen* means here ... to let a thing stand opposed as an object [*das Entgegenstehenlassen des Dinges als Gegenstand*].**

There is a coincidence in the German words he uses: to let *X* stand over against us (*entgegen-stehen*) is to have it for an object (*Gegen-stand*), and that is what representing (*Vor-stellen*, literally, "setting-before") does. Letting *X* stand over against us is not adding any positive feature or quality to *X*, but it is not a negligible thing either, for it is on account of this that *X* can assume the status of object. The position the thing has – to be an object, to be over against us – is defined with reference to the presenter. "Against" (*gegen*) or "over against" (*entgegen*) is certainly a correlation to me or to whoever is doing the presenting, even though this act is nothing more than a *letting*: letting *X* stand over against us (*Entgegen-stehen-lassen*) aims to add no positive feature: such is the force of *lassen*. For *X* to be an object means that we can assign properties to it, expressed in predicates: the coin *is round;* Captain Novus *rescued six sailors*. That allows *X* to be compared with, and contrasted to, other objects that are not round or that performed no heroic deeds.

An Open Interval (ein offenes Entgegen)

But now we ask, what are the conditions for this letting-stand-over-against? The analysis of presentation leads Heidegger to a factor that is a condition for all *Entgegen-stehen*, but that cannot have been created by it. This is an opening, or an open region (*Offenes*). This idea will recur often in Heidegger, in his later accounts of thinking, of dwelling on the earth, and even in his account of time and space; but here we want to appraise its relation to the presenting that is involved in a simple statement, "The coin is round." The initial condition for the presenting is an interval where the presenter and the object stand over against each other, that is called here the *Entgegen* (nominalizing the earlier expression *Entgegenstehenlassen*). Precisely this interval is the condition for the status of *Gegenstand* that is enjoyed by the coin and by the sea captain. In the absence of such an interval there could be no presenting. Nevertheless, precisely *as* being thus placed (over against the presenter), this object has a double action: it accomplishes a movement toward the presenter through the interval, yet, as we read, it stands fast in itself, showing itself unmoved. We read:

> **As thus placed, what stands opposed must traverse an open field of opposedness [*ein offenes Entgegen*] and nevertheless must maintain its stand as a thing and show itself as something withstanding [*ein Ständiges*].**

What is actually accomplished in this traversal, *Durchmessen*, which we might express as "cutting-through"? It does not bump into the presenter or merge with the presenter, because it stands fast. Let us look further into the conditions asserted here for presenting. The zone of the Over-against, *das Entgegen* that we call the Interval, lies within a bigger zone: an Openness or Opening. We can see from the quotation that comes next that this Opening preceded the Interval, the Interval only coming to be as a zone within it:

> **This appearing of the thing in traversing a field of opposedness takes place within an open region, the openness of which is not first created by the presenting but rather is only entered into and taken over as a domain of relatedness.**

We note that the very openness of the Interval was not created by the presenting, the *Vor-stellen*; Heidegger says that the *Vor-stellen* enters into this open – which pre-exists it – and that, for the *Vor-stellen*, the openness has the character of a *Bezugsbereich*, that is, a domain that fosters relationships. The principal relationship of interest here is the one between presenting and coin. We already saw in the previous quotation that the thing or object too entered into the open, and cut through into the Interval – here this is called its appearing, *Erscheinen des Dinges*.

Thus the "traversing" accomplished by the object is the action that is governed by this duality: it means cutting through (*Durchmessen*) into the Interval, but at the same time maintaining its position within the Opening. In the Interval, it is the object, *Gegenstand*, but its more primordial being is as Thing within the Opening. The Interval lies within the Opening, and the gulf or space *within* the Interval, between presenter and object, is one portion of the Opening. The sentence we have quoted affirms the entry of the thing into the Interval; but in the next sentence Heidegger explains that, in our presenting, we too enter into the Interval but do not create it.

Conduct (das Verhalten)

Still reading from **2.2**: Heidegger indicates another step in the meditation that is of the highest consequence. It is through our conduct, *Verhalten*, here translated comportment, that we first form our relation to the opening, or open region; it is not initially through either speech or representation that we occupy the opening.

> **All conduct is distinguished by the fact that, standing in the open region, it in each case adheres to something opened up as such.**

Our encounter with the coin was not initially through presenting it, or making it an object; it was through using it to make payments. In the terminology of *Being and Time*, the daily commerce with coins treats them not as objects but as *Zeug* or *Zuhandenes*, which we may translate as *pragmata*, items of our *praxis* (SZ, p. 68). It is the special point of conduct here that it is *offenständig*, standing open for the thing: through the *Offenständigkeit des Verhaltens* we form a relation to the open zone. This links us not only to the Interval, for the character of our openness is also to be open to whatever may appear in the open domain we have entered. Heidegger, bearing our finitude in mind, recognizes that our opening into the open region of the world cannot occur without an equivalent openness of the various things that occur in the midst of this open region beyond our immediate object. If in our presenting of objects we enter the Interval or *Entgegen*, we nevertheless have already, beforehand, occupied the Opening because of our conduct.

We remember that Heidegger stressed in *SZ* 44 (b) that the uncoveredness, *Entdecktheit*, of the picture hanging on the wall was secondary to the uncovering accomplished by *Da-sein* through statements, perceptions, and conduct. He also argued that the ultimate condition of all truth is the disclosedness, *Erschlossenheit*, of *Da-sein* itself and its world, in a rigorous exercise of his earlier phenomenology, But it soon began to seem to him that *SZ* had stopped short in its questioning regarding these "objects" uncovered by *Da-sein*. The self-showing or unconcealedness of things tends to be overshadowed by the account in Section 44(a) of *Dasein*'s uncovering. If I can objectify a picture on the wall and call it "askew," nevertheless the prior condition for that is that the very shape of the picture frame should be defined (as rectangular, perhaps), and further that that picture's own subject and composition must define the appropriate hanging (suitable to this room, for instance). *SZ* fell short of a fuller account of the self-showing of things in the world. If *Dasein*'s uncovering had primacy over the uncoveredness of the thing (SZ, p. 220), that would not give the full account of the thing's self-showing, whereby it is a phenomenon. Here we see what is perhaps the major advance of *WW* over *SZ*.

One might be tempted to offer a Kantian interpretation of this idea of the *Gegenstand* dwelling in its sphere, the Interval, contrasted with the Thing, the *Ding*, that is seemingly close to a thing-in-itself – thus re-creating the ground of the division of everything into phenomena and *noumena*. But Heidegger does not establish a metaphysical dichotomy of that sort. The coin is at once object and thing; the Interval and the Opening converge and collaborate. The question arises: can this object which is also a thing have a definite identity? Can the Interval and the Opening have a single intelligible character? This will be treated in Units 4 and 5.

There is an appropriateness of response to this conduct: we use the coin in *Such* a way *As* (*So-Wie*) it would require of anyone: this is a directive that is called "inner," meaning that it informs and guides the conduct. *Auftrag* means command, commission, order, usually thought of as imposed by an authority, but here imposed by the humblest little thing, a coin. The conduct accomplishes an adequation to the thing by assimilating this directive imposed by the thing. The conduct is the *Such* –, while the directive gives the *As* –. But all conduct can be appropriate or inappropriate, and we find that just making a statement is already conduct enough.

Looking at the last two sentences of **2.2**, we find that when the thing is *offenbar* and the conduct is *offenständig*, our presentative statement can submit to the directive to express that which is *just as it is*. The role of the Open is not just to foster any sort of awareness of that thing lying there, but to account for the *truth* of the statements we make. The presenting of a thing lets it stand over against us: one zone is formed within the Open. But the Open also appears *within* the Interval! Our conduct reaches into the Open, and the thing is *offenbar* in the Open and is *present* there in advance of its subsequent appearance in the Interval. The Open and the Interval embrace each other, as surely as our conduct and our presentation embrace each other.

The phenomenological study in chapter 2 does not attain to a full explanation of this Opening – it will remain a theme of thinking right through chapter 3 and into the first part of chapter 4, where its character will be more fully charted. Although the reader might be inclined to identify it as Space (or indeed as Space-Time), that would not be adequate, even though the Opening does have some space-like and time-like character. It will be for a later chapter to say wherein consists *die Offenheit dieses Offenen.* Because the object stands in this open Interval, it is something "opened up as such," that is, *ein Offenbares als ein solches*, which could equally be translated as something manifest or revealed. The Interval receives its open zone because of its position within the broader Opening, which was not first constituted by the *Vor-stellen.*

3. The Standard and the Directive: *WW* 2.4–3.1

In the concluding paragraphs of chapter 2, Heidegger spoke of the "standard," *Richtmass*, that guides the presentative correspondence – "**Open comportment [conduct] must let itself be assigned this standard**" (**2.4**) – that emanates from the coin or whatever object is being assumed.

So it is described as a pre-given standard (*Vorgabe des Richtmasses*); "pre-" means in advance of the statement. We assimilate the standard through our conduct and then pass it along from conduct to presentation, and to a statement: the conduct "pre-gives" the standard to the statement.

Next we find a double-barrelled question at the opening of **3.1** that has been split in two in the translation: (1) How can a standard, *eine Richte*, become normative for a statement and given in advance of it? (2) By what means can a statement be guided into its accord, its *Stimmen*? This is also asking why such a process takes place at all: Why do the conduct and the statement conform to an object at all? A statement that presents an object has received a directive, *Weisung*, to conform to that object, *sich richten*, and thus to accord in the fashion of *Richtigkeit*, correctness. So: quite apart from the object's binding standard (*Richtmass*), there seems to be a directive, *Weisung*, that enjoins that we ought to guide ourselves by the object's *Richtmass*. But where did *that* directive come from? It cannot be the thing itself, the round coin, that prescribes for us the directive to conform to objects of whatever description.

We have seen, then, that the *Auftrag* of 1930 has become divided into two in the published versions: there is a measure, *Mass*, and there is a directive, *Weisung*, and they play quite distinct roles. In **2.3**, we read, **"beings present themselves along with the presentative statement so that the latter subordinates itself to the directive, *Weisung*, that it speak of beings *such-as* they are.**" We shall be asking in this unit about the source or authorization of this directive.

The conduct "**must take over a pre[-]given standard for all presenting.**" (*Es muss eine Vorgabe des Richtmasses für alles Vorstellen übernehmen.*) Though the thing puts forward some aspect that serves as a standard, *Richtmass*, the thing's standard could never become authoritative for the statement by itself – that must be mediated by the conduct. The conduct that responds to the *Richtmass* is also what guides the selection of aspects that, in our predicating statement, we choose to assign to the object: "The coin is *round*." But the directive that has become interior to the conduct is not only a specific standard or *Mass* (a coin can be rolled because it is round). There is an open-ended, general directive that we need to become engaged with (*Sich-Einspielen*) the thing towards which we conduct ourselves, and this is the *Weisung*.

The distinction we have just drawn affords a basis for replying to Tugendhat's criticism of *WW*.[126] After the lengthy criticism of *SZ* that takes up the second half of his book, he appends a brief criticism of *WW*; though it is consistent with his whole argument, it can be understood on its own. His general view is that Heidegger never took sufficient notice of the bi-valence of True and False, evident in his tendency to understand truth as "disclosure" or *Erschlossenheit*, where the factor of the False more or less disappeared from view, and thereby "truth" lost its principal meaning. As for *WW*, he notes with approval that Heidegger introduces the *Mass* or standard whereby our statements are to be measured, for this is just what the concept of truth requires, and where its exclusion of the False could take effect (p. 315). Nevertheless, Tugendhat argues (p. 374) that *WW* does not adhere to an effective doctrine of the standard; instead, it resolves the standard into a generalized openness: Heidegger is so concerned with openness that he doesn't allow for how the singular thing actually is, what serves to discriminate true statements from false.[127] In reply, I'd say it is clear from Heidegger's text that the standard or measure (*Mass*) for our statements appears within the Open, but is specifically attached to the singular thing: it is the roundness of the coin that measures our statement, eliminating every other shape as non-applicable, as false.

As for the *Weisung*, it is the belonging-together of conduct and that to which it directs itself. That is the source of the directive, *Weisung*, that we ought to conform our conduct and our statements to that which is – put another way, the directive springs not from the world, but from our insertion in the world, or our being-in-the-world: a worldless subject could not be free, being entirely alone and autonomous. The later pathway, by identifying both the standard and the directive, has improved upon the 1930 version. There, in Unit 3, we noted the role of the *Auftrag*, directive, stemming from the thing and directing first the conduct and then the speaking. But that account was too simple.

In the interest of comprehending the truth of a statement, Heidegger has offered a phenomenology of experience: what makes possible the accordance of a statement with a thing is the interaction of the Open, the traversing and the conduct. Their intimate, intense interaction is the wellspring of the true statement. The statement as such originates from the same matrix as does truth. The analysis does not treat the statement as a neutral entity, either true or false. That would belong to a non-phenomenological form of thinking – phenomenology, rather, traces the origin of utterance to truth itself. Heidegger will turn to questions about falsity and other kinds of untruth only at a later point in the study. Of course, there are things that fall outside our own experience and despite that are the subject of true statements: "Caesar was killed in the Capitol." But here Heidegger has not attempted to account for them, nor for general "truths" (water is composed of hydrogen and oxygen) or mathematical "truths."

If it was an "open-standing conduct" that pinpointed for us the standard, the *Mass*, that pertained to truth – in this case, the round shape of the coin – we may ask further what that implies about the truth of the statement. We can take the occasion to contrast his analysis with the two positions that were taken during a debate in Oxford between J.L. Austin and Peter Strawson.[128] The example: "The cat is on the mat." In a purely grammatical analysis, Austin argued that when a statement was framed in accordance with the conventions governing demonstrative terms (e.g., "this cat"; "that mat"), then the statement would be true if the descriptive conventions of the language ("cat" = such and such a creature; "on the mat" = such and such a position) were also fulfilled in the given case. Austin's claim was that, when we call a statement true, we are asserting that the statement has fulfilled both sets of conventions. Strawson, however, contended that saying a statement is true is not to state something *about* it. We cannot grasp truth through a grammatical analysis – we require another approach that I would call rhetorical (though Strawson does not use that term). To say "S is true" is a completely different kind of speech act, not informative or constative but rather an expression of agreement, endorsement, just like saying "Yes," or "You bet."

The central point here is that neither author needed to make any foray into the phenomenology of experience. We can emphasize the contrast by imagining how Heidegger might have treated the same example. On some fleeting occasion – cats are mobile – you may see that your cat is on the mat and tell that to your wife. With cats, the point of interest is usually *where* they are. Thus the location of the cat is the measure, *Mass*, both for your interaction with the cat and for your statement. The cat has become your object, standing, or sitting, over against you in the Interval. The older condition for that position is that the cat has entered into the Open, and, moreover that you too have entered into the Open, though not merely on this occasion when you made the cat your object, but from the earliest days onward, ever since you acquired the cat and have cared for it. The statement's truth, then, arises from this matrix that includes your conduct, the Open, the Interval for an object, and the standard or measure for both interaction and the statement. Such a phenomenology does not attempt to specify the criterion for the truth of a singular statement ("The coin is round"; "The cat is on the mat") but rather to clarify how in all cases truth comes into being. The ordinary-language approach of Austin and Strawson has no interest in the origin or grounding of truth – the interest is merely to articulate what a speaker *means* in everyday discourse in calling some statement or other true.

4. Presence and Being: *WW* 2.2

Heidegger tells us, at the end of **2.2**, that what is opened up in this way was experienced (*erfahren*) in early Western thinking as "what is present [*das Anwesende*]." This reference to *das Anwesende* is drawing upon Heidegger's studies in early Greek philosophy. "That which is present" is the translation of *to paron* (or, archaically, *to pareon*), the participle of *pareinai*;[129] such a thing embodies *parousia*, presence. So the first question we need to address is: where is this presence achieved? What is its locus? On this point our text is clear: *das Anwesende* is present in the Open, for thereby it has become "opened up as such." Because it is opened up, while present in the Open, our conduct is able to attach itself to it (*sich anhalten*). So it will be vital for us to continue to probe into the origin and composition of this "Open."

To say that the ancients *experienced* what was opened up as *das Anwesende* has several implications. First of all, it does not mean that they *understood* the matter in precisely the way Heidegger has explained – in particular, one should not suppose that they grasped the Open as a function of *Da-sein*, or indeed that they had any grasp of *Da-sein* at all.

If Heidegger stresses that the early Greeks *experienced* that which is present, does that imply that they had as well an experience of the very *presence* of that which is present? The answer is Yes. If something was experienced as *anwesend*, that did not mean, merely, that they saw it or heard it. It meant, rather, that its manifestness was understood to belong to it by nature, owing to its position in the Open. Of itself it was present in and to the Open. This experience was the exposure of the ancients to the Open, which for them was the cosmos, *To Pan* (in chapter 4, Heidegger will identify it as *physis*). The wonder of the ancients was awakened by the experience that the things of the cosmos had accomplished an *arrival* into the Open. Now chapter 2 is not mainly about ancient thought, of course – it is analysing our experience in modern phenomenological terms. Still, Heidegger was right to introduce the ancient experience, for it is echoed in one aspect of the modern setting. In modern phenomenology, we cannot identify the Open as the cosmos or *To Pan* of antiquity; it is instead the *Da* of *Da-sein*. Nevertheless, there is a presence of things in this *Da* that recalls their presence in the ancient cosmos.

How does Heidegger characterize that which is in the Open, that which has been opened up, and that which was experienced by the ancients as *das Anwesende*? He says, at the end of **2.2**, that it has long been named "that which *is* [*das Seiende*]." This identification expresses a long-standing commitment of Heidegger regarding Greek philosophy, that *to* *pareon* or *to paron* affords the meaning of the phrase *to on* (or *to eon*) that we know from Parmenides, Plato, and Aristotle, what has been translated as *das Seiende*.[130] And thus Heidegger's mantra that the *ousia* of the Greek philosophers is to be understood as *parousia*.

At this point in the text, the translator Sallis has rendered *das Seiende* as "being." In the paragraph that follows and in chapter 4, he uses the plural "beings," although the German text employs the same singular term throughout. *Das Seiende* is a participial term signifying whatever in any way *is*, so in practice it would usually indicate a plurality of beings. At this point in *WW*, we have not yet seen *das Sein*, the gerund term formed from the infinitive *sein* – it will make its appearance in **6.2**, and Sallis will render it (as many translators have done) with a capital letter: "Being." But in my text, I shall use the term "being" to translate *das Sein*, and I render *das Seiende* either as "that which is" or as "beings."

Heidegger said at the end of *WW* **2.2** that the *offenbar* was *experienced* in ancient times as "that which is present," he then added that it was *named* "that which is," a name that continues in use even within phenomenology. So what conclusion can we draw from this paragraph regarding *that which is*? Questions of meaning and syntax and translation are particularly urgent with this topic. *Das Seiende* is the name for what has become present within the Open and become manifest, yielding up standards for our conduct, our presenting, and our statements. And this name is the one that remains decisive for thinking and philosophy that recognizes how what-is has achieved presence within the Open. Among the Greeks, the name *to on* was the principal means by which the intellect got hold of the phenomenon. The name also had wider reverberations within the language, within the whole system of the verb: *ta essomena*, what will be; *eimi*, I am; *esti*, he, she, it is; *einai*, to be; and so on. The words all occur at essential places in the writings of Parmenides, Plato, and Aristotle, as vehicles for the key questions of philosophy. Their thinking used these words to make *das Anwesende* intelligible to the mind: it became interpreted as *ousia*, and then further characterized via *eidos*, essence, *hypokeimenon*, and so on. Modern phenomenology also seeks to characterize *das Anwesende*, first as "that which is," then with further interpretations, which are different from those of ancient metaphysics, as we shall see. It is vital not to confuse Heidegger's reference to the *experience* of presence with the *naming function* of *to on*.

But this point must lead us into a discussion of the "new paradigm" for reading Heidegger that has been proposed by Thomas Sheehan. Heidegger's idea of presence, or *Anwesen*, plays a central role in his paradigm.[131] The main current running through his book is the claim that, when Heidegger himself talks about "being," we should read this in every case as "meaningful presence,"[132] the "meaningful presence" of things within the world of our work and engagement, and he regularly tags this with the word *Anwesen*. To discuss his interpretation, I shall draw on some recent discussions, including two books by Capobianco,[133] and recent posts by him and others on the Heidegger Circle website.

A characteristic reference comes early on to "the *Anwesen* of things – that is, their meaningful presence within the worlds of human interests and concerns, whether those be theoretical, practical, aesthetic, religious, or whatever."[134] Later passages express the same idea in various ways: "meaningfully present to us within our concerns and performances" (p. 10); "meaningful presence of something in and for human intelligence" (p. 32); and many other variations. Any talk of "presence" such as the Greeks practised needs to invoke "an interested 'dative,' an involved 'recipient' of that presence"; it is necessarily "presence *unto*" (p. 35). For Sheehan, there is no doubt that the recipient of this *Anwesen* is the existing *Dasein*, our "interests and concerns," our intelligence and performances. Sheehan backs up his point with a stress on *phenomenology* as the philosophical method.[135] The theme of meaning is the whole *métier* of phenomenology, he says – see the opening of his chapter 4 ("Meaningfulness is the mostly unnoticed dimension through which alone I can encounter whatever shows up": p. 111), and the closing of the same chapter ("We live in meaningful contexts, worlds of meaning shaped by our interests and concerns, which confer meaning on the things that inhabit those contexts": p. 131). But on page 10 Sheehan accepts Aron Gurwitsch's conception of phenomenology as entirely devoted to meaning; this is different from Heidegger's own conception of phenomenology as expressed in *SZ*, Section 7 – which Sheehan does not mention at all – where *das Sein* is the principal phenomenon.[136]

The broader reaches of this name – *ousia, das Sein* – make it quite inappropriate to *reduce* being to presence. His paradigm says that when Heidegger himself talks about being, we should read this in every case as "meaningful presence."[137] If "presence," such as the Greeks practised, needs to invoke "an interested 'dative,' an involved 'recipient' of that presence" (p. 35), so Sheehan argues, *we must also grant the "dative" in the case of "being."* His conception is particularly opposed to a realist ontology that attempts to discuss "Being" as a substance apart from human involvement (p. 127), and Sheehan maintains that Heidegger's readers have all too often attributed to him such an ontology – of big "B," a "super-*Sein*" (p. 19) – what is just "out there," that we "bump into" (p. 127). Against all that, he says that Heidegger accomplished an interpretation of Aristotle that displaced the traditional "realist" readings and showed the phenomenological achievements of Aristotle (pp. 105–6).

(On this last point I am in accord – this was indisputably a great achievement on Heidegger's part.)

But now, in *WW* chapters 1–3, what is the force of Sheehan's paradigm? Where he wants to say that being is meaningful presence, we must ask, regarding *WW*, chapter 2, whether *something significant is added* when "that which is present" is given the additional name "that which *is*." Or is being just presence, after all? We may notice a crucial omission from Sheehan's own account of presence. It concerns the *location* of the presence of *das Seiende*. Heidegger makes it clear that it is present *in the Open*, because these beings acquire openness by being present there – they are opened up. But this all becomes foreshortened in Sheehan's account, which assumes that the beings are simply present *to Da-sein*, what he calls the "dative" of their presence-to. We approached this question in Unit 2 above when we asked whether there is a single intelligible identity to be assigned to the "object" in the Interval and the "thing" in the Open. The answer is that it is *das Seiende*, that which is. Insofar as *das Seiende* is present in the Open, it does not exhaust itself in being present, *qua* object, in the Interval. For Sheehan, the human being (*Da-sein* in the ontic sense) is the term for this presence.

But there is another motif as well running through Sheehan's book, which I might call revisionist. Sheehan criticizes fifty years of scholarship that focused on the theme of being in Heidegger. Opposing this, he is led to say that Heidegger's philosophy was not about being at all, but rather about sense or meaning (p. xi). Where Heidegger speaks of "being itself," that is not any kind of *Sein* at all (p. xv). He particularly disputes older commentators like de Waehlens and his many followers (pp. 149–50). This negative thrust predominates in the opening pages of his book – getting rid of being. Then Sheehan turns his polemic against Heidegger himself (pp. xiv–xvi, 3–9): Heidegger, he contends, was in a state of confusion, not knowing what he wanted to say when he spoke about being. On pages 4–9, Sheehan gives us a list of about sixty phrases drawn from Heidegger's writings, which together seem intended to show that the discourse about being produces an irreconcilable, chaotic proliferation of ideas. But Sheehan did not take the trouble to interpret any of these expressions, or to compare them in detail – if, instead of just conflating isolated utterances from all periods and from all genres, he had interpreted them and compared them, we might have gained new insights into Heidegger.

In making explicit reference to *das Seiende* as that which shows itself in the Open, and in the Over-against, the text is correcting the earlier focus on the a priori *Seinsverständnis* that guides the sciences. The thing that lies in the open, the object that stands in the Over-against, and that which is present – they are all identified as *das Seiende*. But what is the grounding for this last designation? What constitutes the *being* of these beings that we encounter? It is rooted in the encounter that sustains the essence of truth. The thing or object yields a standard to which conduct, representation, and statements all conform. But we conform to the standard because we are also constrained by the directive (*Weisung)* to conform all our intentions to that which *is*. The constraint arises from our insertion in the world, our being in the world. Occupying as we do a position in the world, we cannot deny to the thing its own, equal footing in the world, for it is out of that belonging that it has accomplished its own entry into the open. That belonging and that entry together constitute its being.

5. Freedom and Letting-Be: *WW* 4.1–4.4

Now to turn to the more complex account of freedom offered in 1949. Our conduct, and therefore our statements, are led into their conforming because we have taken up a position in the open – as we have already seen. Now we read in **3.1**: The "**pregiving [conduct] has already entered freely into an open region for something opened up that prevails there and that binds every presenting**." Here we locate Heidegger's later view of freedom, which was already expressed in the term we have used here, *Offenständigkeit des Verhaltens*, "the standing-open of conduct [comportment]." This implies standing-open-*to*-something, or as he also says in this paragraph, being-free-*for*-something. **"To free oneself for a binding directedness is possible only by being free for what is opened up in an open region."** He does not think of freedom as a competence or property of the subject, our capacity to turn this way or that. Freedom depends on a relation *to* something which is encountered in an open sphere.

A crucial modification must now be recognized regarding the human being. As he put it in 1930, **"The human being is not the bearer and possessor of freedom and truth, but everything is the other way around"** (*GA* 80, p. 390). I do not think that in 1930 Heidegger accomplished the reversal he intended in these lines – but he was able to accomplish it in the 1949 version.

The freedom he is speaking of is not the human being's possession of a manifold of possibilities. If someone possessed many possibilities – to steal a coin, to melt it down, to spend it – then these could be merely the projection of inner drives, the immanent possibilities of the human organism. The possession of such a set of possibilities could not constitute a foundation for correctness about a coin. But it would not afford a proper grasp of freedom either. What is required for either correctness or freedom is the openness for a possibility that is *not* posited purely through the development of whatever drives and forces pertain to the human organism. For someone to be free, it requires that he/she has moved out into a zone that, because it is open per se, opens up possibilities that are not anticipated in any inner drives. Freedom is often thought to be liberation from some confinement, but those drives and forces themselves are the most elementary confinement, from which we are delivered through venturing into the open zone. Freedom is a relationship, letting-be, not an interior property of the human being.

We are then able to say that the freedom that constitutes the essence of truth is, in its own essence, the very same thing as the Open that we saw earlier, in which the Interval between statement and thing was hovering. The 1930 version did not quite get to the point of establishing that identity – it remained more subjectively oriented, assigning freedom to the conduct and intentions of the human being. Both versions, though, connect freedom essentially to our letting the beings be.

I want to emphasize that this stage of the inquiry has not changed the subject, away from truth and turning to freedom. We are instead going deeper into the essence of truth by asking why anyone is in search for truth in the first place.

We have seen that conduct apprehends a standard and then passes it along to a presentation, and to a statement: the conduct "pre-gives" the standard to the statement. But Heidegger's first question in chapter 3 was why such a process takes place at all. Each mode of conduct does experience the binding force emanating from the thing – the repair of an implement needs to be guided by what the thing ought to be. This is the revealing that lets the conduct correspond. Wealready read in 1930:

> **But what does that mean, that the conduct that relates itself to something must beforehand have revealed that being as a being? Nothing less than that the conduct must, in advance, have let that being be just the being that it is, and in the way that it is. A being could never have become revealed as a being, whether as an object or otherwise, if the conduct towards it had not already held to the stance of letting the being be.** (quoting from 1930, p. 391)

Now these points are treated in more detail, in **4.1** and. **4.2.** That letting-be is the essence of freedom. The conduct is receiving its directive, so the corresponding stance of the conduct towards the thing is *letting it be.* The revealing of a being through any mode of our conduct could not occur unless the conduct adhered to the stance of letting the being be. We might expand here on the idea of freedom, looking ahead to his remarks in chapter 4 on negative and positive freedom:

> **Freedom is not merely what common sense is content to let pass under that name: the caprice, turning up occasionally in our choosing, of inclining in this or that direction. Freedom is not mere absence of constraint with respect to what we can or cannot do. Nor is it on the other hand mere readiness for what is required and necessary (and so somehow a being). Prior to all this ("negative" and "positive" freedom), freedom is engagement in the disclosure of beings as such. Disclosedness itself is conserved in ek-sistent engagement, through which the openness of the open region, i.e., the "there" ["*Da*"] is what it is. (*WW* 4.4)**

Heidegger highlights his view of freedom by contrasting it with two other concepts. The negative version is close to commonsense views – "mere absence of constraint with respect to what we can and cannot do" – but it has also found philosophical expression over the centuries; in his lectures in 1930,[138] Heidegger documented this negative concept in Kant's *Grounding for the Metaphysics of Morals*, especially the Third Section. By contrast, "positive freedom" is not native to our common sense and has been rather a theme promoted by some philosophers: "the readiness for what is required and necessary." Heidegger's distinction seems to be the same as the one made familiar to English-speaking readers by Berlin in his "Two Concepts of Liberty," a lecture from 1958.[139] This concept of a positive freedom is often ascribed to such authors as Rousseau and Hegel, but in the 1930 lectures[140] Heidegger showed that there was a positive freedom in Kant as well, when Kant attempted to prove, in the same text quoted, that a free will and a will subject to the moral law were one and the same. Heidegger's letting-be stands in contrast to both these concepts because it is "prior" to them, or more original – as the very event in which beings become manifest to us. This original freedom is a self-engagement with beings (*Sicheinlassen auf das Seiende*) at the opening of **4.3**, and is subsequently called a *Sicheinlassen auf das Offene und dessen Offenheit.* And in **4.4** this reflexive term is modified into something less voluntaristic: *Eingelassenheit in die Entbergung des Seienden*, being-admitted-into.

In *WW*, chapter 4, we discover an account of freedom that brings us closer to the theme of being. Freedom is exhibited as the "letting-be of beings," *Seinlassen des Seienden.* Here we have the power of *Da-sein* recognized – to let the beings be: *Seinlassen des Seienden* is undertaken and to be accomplished by *das Da-sein*, and although we are thereby thrust into the Open of *das Da*, it is the very *sein* of *das Da-sein* that is the agent of letting-be. The *Seinlassen* is accomplished through our conduct, *Verhalten.* The *sein* of *das Da-sein* is certainly a self-surpassing, a perpetual exiting from self – thrust into the *Da* – whereby the letting-be of that which is is accomplished. But, crucially, that is not presence.

But Sheehan, we have seen, completely identifies being with presence. The implication is that, just as presence requires the "dative" that is the human being, so too *we must grant the "dative" in the case of "being."* Sheehan invokes the counter-example of remote geological ages, prior to the emergence of humanity, asserting that we cannot assign Heidegger's "being" to such ages in which humanity was absent (p. 11). This problem that he has posed for himself only arises, of course, given that he insists on identifying being with presence, that is, presence to *Da-sein.* A further oddity of his treatment is that it avoids any treatment of the being of this *Da-sein* itself: the *Sein* of *Da-sein* cannot be understood by way of presence to this *Da-sein.* Here Sheehan is looking away from Heidegger's major subject. *Da-sein*'s letting-be is the root of both conduct and presentation, and it is letting-be that affords our access to the beings that have achieved their presence in the Open. Just as these beings can then become our objects in the Interval, so our presentations and statements take their own origin from our letting-be.

In these expressions we have mention not only of the factor of beings – in the word *SEINlassen,* we also have the verbal infinitive *sein.* One must seek to understand this *sein* – it is in no way vulnerable to Sheehan's critique of the traditional ontology of substance. Let us consider our experience of cooperation, a joint interaction of both of us with the environment. If, for instance, two of us cooperate in the maintenance of a house, there is a joint operation of *Seinlassen,* whereby one single *Seiendes,* the house, is engaged by the double letting-be of both persons. The care they combine to offer is focused on the fabric of the house, its suitability for dwelling, its value, its endurance, its safety, its location, its past history and its future, its legal and economic status. These items of concern impinge on the *being* of the house, for they are governed by its status: it is "our home"; or it is "our property"; or it is "our investment" or "our inheritance"; or it is "your mother's home." True, the house offers itself to view in its *Anwesen,* its presence, but it is only in a wider view that one can say *what it is.* Because it is *Seiendes,* it continues to call forth innumerable variants of letting-be from innumerable persons who embody the force of *Da-sein* in themselves. Such a *Seiendes* can then become the occasion of a true statement.

We may treat this matter less formally or abstractly by taking cognizance of the fact that, for each of us, other human beings are the most prominent cases of *das Seiende,* even though in *WW* we are all constituted by the common essence or grounding, *das Da-sein.* In relation to other human beings we all experience the most important expression of letting (other) beings be, *Seinlassen des Seienden:* in encouraging your projects, caring for your welfare, accepting the results of your initiatives, I am giving expression to *das Da-sein* in me by letting you be. Where the other *Seiendes* is another human being incarnating *Da-sein*, the *Sein* of the other *Da-sein* cannot be understood as simple presence. We recognize in the others the very same transcending power and freedom that we have ourselves – *Da-sein ist ein Wesen der Ferne*, marked by absence as much as by presence. We can repeat here the point from the end of Unit 4, that *Da-sein's* recognition of the being of beings cannot be construed along the lines of an *a priori* projection of being.

In conclusion, then, being cannot be reduced to presence – for Heidegger, that was true only of the Greeks, and was a limitation suffered by their thought. Heidegger says in chapter 99 of *WW* 1949 that this essay had not attempted to discuss the being of beings, and we must respect this limitation, but in Unit 12 below we shall return to this point, asking what is implied on that question by the present pathway of thought.

6. Unconcealedness in the Later Heidegger: *WW* 4.3–4.5

In 1949, at the end of chapter 3, Heidegger allowed an antagonist to give voice to objections – essentially the same ones we rehearsed earlier in Part I, Unit 5, though in more analytical detail, and he found that these objections rested upon three preconceptions: (a) there is no need to inquire any further into the constitution of freedom; (b) everyone already knows well enough what a human being is; (c) in any case, freedom has to be a property or attribute of the human being.

Chapter 4 will now advance a form of thinking that will overthrow these prejudices, launching an inquiry into "The Essence of Freedom" (its title).

Here we have the 1949 revision of Section II(a), no. 2:

> **The phrase that we now need – "letting beings be" – does not refer to neglect and indifference but rather the opposite. To let be is to engage oneself with beings. On the other hand, to be sure, this is not to be understood only as the mere management, preservation, tending, and planning of the beings in each case encountered or sought out. To let be – that is, to let beings be as the beings that they are – means to engage oneself with the open region and with its very openness, where all the beings have entered in and taken their stand – for they are always accompanied by this openness [*das jene gleichsam mit sich bringt*]. Western thinking in its beginning conceived the open region as *ta alēthea*, the unconcealed.**

This introduces the Unconcealed, *das Unverborgene* and *die Unverborgenheit.* All that we have reviewed in *WW* **2** and **3** was expressed originally in the Greek words *ta alēthea* and *alētheia.* In *WW*, chapter 2, we made the acquaintance with an *Entgegen* that was also open, and that derived its openness from the broader domain, an open region that we entered with our comportment and that the thing entered. In the interval, this Open was the gap between presenting and thing, or between word and object. Only now in chapter 4, after considerable argumentation, has Heidegger introduced Greek terminology: the collective term *ta alēthea,* the things that lie unconcealed; and the abstract noun *alētheia,* unconcealedness itself of beings. The original Greek unconcealedness is not introduced here as a curious or antiquarian point: the original encounter with *alētheia* was the beginning of the history in which we still stand. It is authoritative for us.

The issue arises here of the relation between our letting-be and the unconcealedness of beings. In this respect, the present text can be contrasted with the 1930 version. In the corresponding section of 1930, treated above in Part I, Unit 6, it was *Da-sein*'s letting-be that brought about *alētheia,* the unconcealedness of the thing. And as we saw in that Unit, *SZ 44* treated *alētheia* in a similar way. But now, in 1949, the relation is reversed: the open zone, the unconcealed, *alētheia,* must already be constituted if we are to encounter entities in it – their unconcealment is what permits us to let them be. In 1949, the *alētheia* has a direct connection to the beings themselves. My translation of the phrase *das jene gleichsam mit sich bringt* assumes that "beings" are the subject of the verb *bringt* and "openness" the object. But even if it were the other way around – "for the openness always has beings in it" – the *alētheia* would still not be the product of our letting-be.

In the On-Line Forum of the Heidegger Circle,[141] there has been discussion of the relation between *Da-sein* and *alētheia*; some have argued either that they are the same or that *Da-sein* is a condition for *alētheia*; others maintain that *alētheia* is constituted independently of *Da-sein.* With respect to *WW*, we can say that 1930 took the first position, while 1949 took the second (though, to be sure, the present text has not yet begun to use the term *Da-sein* – it appears later in chapter 4).

Besides "unconcealedness," *Unverborgenheit,* as a translation of the Greek term, the text also proposes *Entborgenheit,* which I usually render as "de-conceal." as something that was "still uncomprehended" (both in **4.3** and **4.5**), implying that it had not been grasped by anyone in antiquity, and is still not grasped in our time – it is the task of thinking now to attend to it. While the term "unconcealedness" serves as a translation of *alētheia, entbergen* and *Entborgenheit* are terms that belong to Heidegger's own thought, and the active verb is the important one.[142] In charting these terms among several languages, we should pay heed to the remark in **4.3**:

> **If we translate *alētheia* as "unconcealedness" rather than "truth," this translation is not merely "more literal"; it contains the directive to rethink the ordinary concept of truth in the sense of the correctness of statements and to think it back to that still uncomprehended de-concealedness and de-concealing of beings.**

The early Greeks had had an experience of *alētheia*, but had not comprehended that which lay at the basis of it, which is what Heidegger is calling *Entborgenheit*. Heidegger's thought is attempting to reach into this depth. In the curving pathway of this essay, we have detached truth, not only from the statement, but now also from human conduct. If truth is *alētheia*, it is now assigned to beings – and indeed, in a further step, to *being*. Heidegger continues:

> **To engage oneself with the de-concealedness of beings is not to lose oneself in them; rather, such engagement withdraws in the face of beings in order that they might reveal themselves with respect to what and how they are, and in order that presentative correspondence might take its standard from them.**

Here I offer another comment on Sheehan.[143] In the course of his new paradigm, Sheehan postulates *alētheia* as a central pillar of Heidegger's thought, and he argues (pp. 71–9) that it appears in three main forms. One of them is the unconcealedness or disclosure of beings (Sheehan, pp. xvii, 76–7), which is exemplified in our quotation from *WW*, chapter 4:

> **If we translate *alētheia* as "unconcealment" rather than "truth," this translation is not merely "more literal"; it contains the directive to rethink the ordinary concept of truth in the sense of the correctness of statements and to think it back to that still uncomprehended de-concealedness and de-concealing of beings.**[144]

But this is dependent upon a deeper and older deconcealment, viz. that of being itself, and this is what Sheehen calls *alētheia*-1, distinguished terminologically from the previous case, now called "*alētheia*-2."

But for Sheehan, there is also an *alētheia*-3 (pp. 73–4), the truth of a statement, which, as Heidegger showed in *SZ* 44 and elsewhere, engages in uncovering or disclosing or manifesting or displaying the thing or state of affairs it was about. Although this is a form of *alētheia*, it is here that Sheehan applies his polemical force: it is *only* this last and most derivative form of *alētheia* that deserves the title "truth." "We should reserve the word 'truth' (*Wahrheit*) for such *adaequatio* or correctness and refuse to follow Heidegger in his misleading use of that word for the disclosedness of things (and even worse, for the openedness of ex-sistence)"[145] Heidegger was wrong to assign the term "truth" to the unconcealedness that he introduced in chapter 4, and in all the many works that treat of it.

In reply to Sheehan, I must point out the character of a pathway – it takes its start at some point, and in *WW*, that is the phenomenon of a statement's truth, and the traditional account of such truth (*adaequatio* and correctness). Thinking does not rest complacently in this beginning: the pathway on which it is forced to move will bring us to a range of further phenomena that are discovered from the optic of the way that made this particular start. The pathway of *WW* goes from *adaequatio*, through "*offenständiges Verhalten*," to freedom, to letting-be, then on to the self-manifesting of beings (and it does not stop there!) – all these the mutations undergone by the truth from which we made our start. If, partway through the pathway, we come to unconcealedness, my question must be: How did we get there? In keeping with all philosophy that wants to set the citizen on the right path, we need to be alert to the point at which the path starts, from which the successive phenomena receive their identity. And these instances of *alētheia* should not be separated from one another, as in Sheehan. Heidegger concluded his remark in **4.3** on the deconcealedness or revelation of beings by noting how "the presentative correspondence might take its standard from them."

Now we look at the 1943–49 revision of the topic of *Da-sein*, found in **4.5**:

> **In Da-sein, the essential ground, long ungrounded, on the basis of which human beings are able to ek-sist, is preserved for them. Here "existence" does not mean *existentia* in the sense of occurring or being at hand. Nor, on the other hand, does it mean, in an "existentiell" fashion, the moral endeavor of the human being on behalf of his "self," based on his psychophysical constitution. Ek-sistence, rooted in truth as freedom, is exposure to the disclosedness of beings as such. Still uncomprehended, indeed, not even in need of an essential grounding, the ek-sistence of historical human beings begins at that moment what the first thinker takes a questioning stand with regard to the unconcealment of beings by asking: what are beings? In this question unconcealment is experienced for the first time. Beings as a whole reveal themselves as *physis*, "nature," which here does not yet mean a particular sphere of beings but rather beings as such as a whole,**

specifically in the sense of upsurgent presencing [*aufgehendes Anwesen*]. History begins only when beings themselves are expressly drawn up into their unconcealment and conserved in it, only when this conservation is conceived on the basis of questioning regarding beings as such. The originary disclosure of beings as a whole, the question concerning beings as such, and the beginning of Western history are the same; they occur together in a "time" which, itself unmeasurable, first opens up the open region for every measure.

Heidegger is promising us an experience of the deeper and hidden essential ground of the human being. It is here, for the first time, that he introduces the word *Da-sein,* employing it in a way quite different from his practice in *SZ.* It would be a misunderstanding of the second sentence of the chapter, which introduces *das Da-sein* in parentheses, to think Heidegger was going to probe into the concealed essential ground of *Da-sein;* rather, the latter *is* the essential ground of the human being. In *WW* 1943 and 1949, the distinction between *Mensch* and *Da-sein* is consistently observed. He is introducing *Da-sein* as the hidden, essential grounding of the human being. Indeed we read here (end of **4.4**) first of all about the *"Da,"* the "There," a version of the Opening or the open region that we have heard about since chapter 2. This original Opening became expressed as freedom in chapter 3, and now recurs as the *Da.* The *Da* permits the deconcealedness, *die Entborgenheit,* of beings. What then of *Da-sein,* which is mentioned in the next line, opening **4.5**? We should understand *sein* here as a verb, ideally in the middle voice, to signify: sustaining and being sustained by the *Da. Da-sein* is exposure to deconcealedness (*Aussetzung in die Entborgenheit*); as Heidegger expressed it at the end of **4.3**, "**the essence of freedom is exposure to the deconcealedness of beings.**" The deconcealedness is preserved, and the exposure to it is also preserved, in *Da-sein.* What Heidegger has been calling exposure here now becomes re-expressed as ek-sistence: "Letting-be, i.e., freedom, is intrinsically exposing, ek-sistent." All these are the relationships that sustain the *Da,* the Opening. But all these relationships within the *Da* invoke the character of the deconcealedness, *die Entborgenheit,* that Heidegger said in **4.3** was still uncomprehended in ancient times. Though it was not comprehended then, it was experienced, *erfahren,* and called *alētheia.*

Having charted these relationships, Heidegger is now able to open **4.5** with a restatement of his promised insight:

In *Da-sein,* the essential ground, long ungrounded, on the basis of which human beings are able to ek-sist, is preserved for them.

We need to ask what he intends with the term *Wesensgrund* ("essential ground"). It does not coincide with any of the earlier versions of *Wesen*, because this is the grounding *for* a *Wesen*, where, earlier, an essence was understood to be itself the ground for a possibility. The present grounding is for the human *Wesen*, that is, the grounding is what permits the human being to ek-sist. Thus we should take *wesen* here as a verb – for human being or existing. A few lines down, Heidegger says that human ek-sistence is "**the exposure to the disclosedness of beings as such**," and that such ek-sistence is *rooted* (*gewurzelt*) in truth as freedom – another reference to "grounding"; he could just as well have said it was rooted in *Da-sein*. The sentence we quoted said that this *Wesensgrund* was "**long ungrounded**," *langehin ungegründet*, which is to be understood as "not comprehended." A few lines down we read that the ek-sistence of historical human beings, at the beginning, was "**still uncomprehended, indeed not even in need of a *Wesensgründung*, an essential grounding**." It is the exposure to uncomprehended disclosedness that makes human ek-sistence historical. Being exposed to things gives Heidegger a way of explaining his term *Da-sein*; *Da-sein* is in front of things, and in front of the whole world, exposed. Here our thinking meets the experience as it was lived in history. The ground for the human being is ek-sistent exposure, encounter in the *Da* with every manner of beings, with all the risk, danger, and joy that attend such an adventure. Heidegger's deeper and hidden grounding of the human being makes philosophical materialism, and the *animal rationale*, obsolete and irrelevant.

4.6. It is after this that Heidegger explains why he can say that freedom is not a human attribute, but rather overpowers us. Not our attribute, freedom is now identified both with existence and with the open sphere in which the things and world display themselves. That gives Heidegger further occasion to deny the "commonsense" idea of freedom, as an ability to incline this way or that. "**Freedom, ek-sistent, disclosive *Da*-sein, possesses the human being**." The discussion concludes with a turn again to antiquity.

There is one notable qualification, introduced by a handwritten note that Heidegger added after 1943. His original text read: "**Only the ek-sistent human being is historical. 'Nature' has no history**." The marginal note refers to the first sentence: "**Inadequate. Essence of history in terms of history as *Ereignis*.**" Without attempting a full elucidation of that point here, I might say that some of its sense is captured in another sentence drawn from **4.8**: "**That the human being ek-sists now means that for historical humanity the history of its essential possibilities is conserved in the disclosure of beings as a whole.**"